Praise for *10*

There is constant messaging, whether through programs or principles, around being a healthier version of you. There's a similar message within the American church around revitalization—where churches enter into a gospel process of reversing the downward direction of decline and plateau. Serving as a faithful voice in this area, Karl Vaters writes an excellent revitalization primer full of practical principles for how church leaders can begin leading their church in a healthier direction in just over three months. My encouragement to you would be to eat the words, exercise the principles, and watch your church get healthier.

ED STETZER
Billy Graham Distinguished Chair for Church, Mission, and Evangelism, and Executive Director of the Billy Graham Center for Evangelism, Wheaton College

Reading Karl's *100 Days* is like hiring a consultant to come to your church and walk you through a renewal process. But where you would normally pay thousands of dollars for such a service, Karl pours his decades of expertise and wisdom into the pages of this book—accessible *to* and affordable *for* the small church pastor. If you want to move your church forward, either in mission, programming or overall health, don't just put this book at the top of your must-read list. Put it at the top of your must-do list.

CHRIS VITARELLI
Pastor and author of *Small Church BIG Deal: How to Rethink Size, Success and Significance in Ministry* and founder of the Small Church BIG Deal Conference

If there's another book like this out there, we don't know about it. With crystal clarity, Karl lays out a plan toward greater health that any pastor and church leadership can easily wrap their arms around. There's no guesswork, and there's no gimmick—every day from 1 to 100 includes not only the what but the why and the how. And this is not just a book for struggling churches; it is a heart-check for every church at any stage. *100 Days to a Healthier Church* should be a coffee-stained and dog-eared manual on every pastor's desk.

CARL & KALANI CULLEY
Founders of Big Little Church Conference

I don't know of a better guide than Karl to lead you and your team on a journey to help create a more healthy church. This is a book that should be in every pastor's library. It's thoughtful, thorough, and practical.

TROY MCLAUGHLIN
Project Pastor Podcast

Karl Vaters has done it again! This book will help churches of all different sizes become more intentional about maintaining their spiritual health. If you're serious about growing healthier and expanding your kingdom influence, this book is for you. It is both intensely biblical and practical at the same time. Karl gives us the view from 10,000 feet and the ground level. In today's fast-paced ministry culture, it will force you to slow down and lay a foundation that Jesus Christ will build HIS church on.

MICHAEL J. RUBINO
Cornerstone Bible Church PJS

There are few things in life as encouraging as having a parent, coach, or teacher put their arm around you and point you in the right direction. The essence of each encounter results in a renewed confidence that you can accomplish the task that is before you. In writing *100 Days to a Healthier Church,* Karl Vaters has provided a step-by-step approach of practical principles that will help your ministry to experience *healthy* growth. The best way to get to your desired destination is to be honest about your current situation. As Karl reminds us, the most important step to experience change is to first make the choice to change! My hope is that you will embrace Karl's 30 years of ministry experience by implementing these principles in your ministry over the next 100 days.

DALE SELLERS
Executive Director, 95Network

A tested and proven 15-week process that's manageable, adaptable, and effective. It will be hard to read this book without writing in the margins and underlining the pure gold found on the printed page. The principles included will help you lead your church to health and vitality.

TOM CHEYNEY
Founder & Directional Leader, The Renovate Group
The Church Revitalizer as Change Agent

100 DAYS
—— TO A ——
HEALTHIER
CHURCH

A STEP-BY-STEP GUIDE FOR PASTORS & LEADERSHIP TEAMS

KARL VATERS

MOODY PUBLISHERS

CHICAGO

Edited by Annette LaPlaca
Interior design: Ragont Design and Erik M. Peterson
Cover design: Faceout Studio
Cover photo of garden spade copyright © 2019 by Pinkyone/Shutterstock (134767190). All rights reserved.
Author photo: George Samuel Beaver

Library of Congress Control Number:2019955713

Originally delivered by fleets of horse-drawn wagons, the affordable paperbacks from D. L. Moody's publishing house resourced the church and served everyday people. Now, after more than 125 years of publishing and ministry, Moody Publishers' mission remains the same—even if our delivery systems have changed a bit. For more information on other books and products written and produced from a biblical perspective, go to www.moodypublishers.com or write to:

Moody Publishers
820 N. LaSalle Boulevard
Chicago, IL 60610

1 3 5 7 9 10 8 6 4 2

Printed in the United States of America

To my parents
Albert and Anita Vaters

You have taught me and so many others
by your words and your extraordinary example
what a healthy family and healthy church look like.

Contents

HEALTHY CHANGE
HAPPENS IN COMMUNITY.

Be encouraged by connecting with other pastors and churches going through the 100 Days—find them at

karlvaters.com

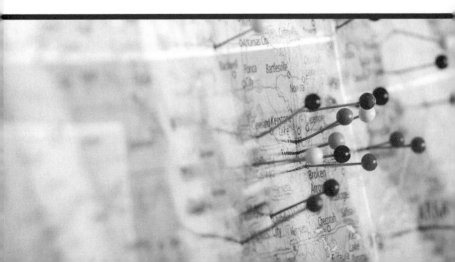

Introduction

R eading this book will be easy.
Doing this book will be hard.

The principles laid out here are not one-time, quick-fix so-lutions. They are long-term principles—nudges, not jumps. It's about being the tortoise, not the hare.

I am profoundly thankful when I hear about a church exploding in growth. But in most churches, growth doesn't happen explosively. It happens little by little, piece by piece, day by day.

DO YOU WANT TO GET WELL?

How much healthier can a church really get in 100 Days?

That depends on a variety of factors, including its current state of health, its history, and more. But one factor is more important than any other, and it goes back to the question Jesus asked the man in John 5:6, "Do you want to get well?"

Jesus said he would build His church. So we know He's committed. He absolutely wants His church to be healthy and strong—and that includes the congregation you serve.

Do *you* want to get well?

Does *your church* want to get well?

The degree to which your church is committed to health

NOTHING PAVES THE WAY FOR SPONTANEITY LIKE THOROUGH PLANNING.

and wellness will be seen in how hard you are willing to work for it.

A healthy church is intentional about everything. Even churches with a free-flowing worship style are better able to make changes when they've been intentional about creating a time and space for it to happen. Though it may seem counterintuitive, nothing paves the way for spontaneity like thorough planning!

Before the 100 Days

*Equip God's people
to do his work.*

Ephesians 4:12 NLT

CHAPTER 1

Get Better before You Get Bigger

Any church can become healthier in 100 Days—not perfect, but healthier.

If a church is especially ill, it may not become *healthy* in 100 Days, but it can be *healthier* than it is right now—as in less sick, and one step closer to becoming the strong, vibrant, effective congregation it was meant to be.

PRINCIPLES, NOT PROMISES

There are no one-size-fits-all methods that will make a church healthier, but there are principles. This book is a reverse-engineering of the principles our church has learned by trial and error over the last two and a half decades of moving from sickness to health, then into deeper levels of effective ministry.

These principles have also been discussed, tested, refined, and taught to thousands of church leaders, proving themselves workable in churches of all styles and sizes.

HOW TO USE THIS BOOK

If you are a pastor or leader of a local congregation, read this book through in its entirety first. Then do a trial run by yourself or with a trusted ministry partner (maybe your spouse). By doing this self-test first, you'll be more prepared to lead the church through the principles later.

If you personalize these principles seriously before teaching others, you can become a healthier church leader in 100 Days, and a church with a healthier leader is a healthier church.

Let me include a quick note about church size. Since the average church worldwide has a Sunday attendance of about seventy-five people, this process is designed with a church of that size in mind. If you're in a church with fewer than fifty (which is about half the churches in the world), some of the instructions about team size will need to be adapted for your smaller congregation. For churches of more than two hundred, remember that most of this book is written with volunteer leaders in mind, so you will need to adapt to include paid staff members. Actually, every church of every size will need to tweak various steps as you walk through this process. That's expected and normal. Methods are meant to be tweaked, but the principles are biblical and universal.

THE HEALTHY CHURCH CONTINUUM

The goal of this book is not to help you start a new program, or pattern your congregation after another successful church. The goal is to take another step toward becoming the church God called you to be.

To begin this process, imagine church health on a continuum of Negative 10 (-10) to Positive 10 (+10).

These are not precise metrics, but they can be a helpful way to imagine different stages of church health and maturity.

Negative 10: A church at this level of ill health is not just ineffective but dangerous and toxic. There have probably been many years of inner conflicts, bad blood, and a poor reputation in the surrounding community.

The first-century Corinthian church was in a similar condition. They had everything from sex scandals to lawsuits to rampant pride about their own tolerance of such sins (1 Cor. 6–7). In fact, the apostle Paul famously told them, "In the following directives I have no praise for you, for your meetings do more harm than good" (1 Cor. 11:17).

Negatives 9 through 1: Churches in this range have various levels of ill health. The New Testament church at Sardis, which was instructed to "Wake up! Strengthen what remains and is about to die" (Rev. 3:1–6) might have been at -8 or -9 on the church health spectrum, while the Ephesian church that had "persevered and . . . endured hardships for my name" but had lost their first love (Rev. 2:1–7) was probably at -2 or -1.

Zero: We'll be sticking with the "unhealthy" label for a church at zero, because even if the people in the church are getting along and having no fights or scandals, a church in neutral is making minimal contributions to Christ's mission on earth.

This was the problem with the lukewarm Laodicean church (Rev. 3:14–22). Their sin was feeling smug about their status. They thought they were getting along well and in need of nothing, but Jesus was ready to spit them out for their lack of passion.

WE'VE BEEN GIVEN A MISSION, AND WE NEED TO TAKE IT SERIOUSLY. DON'T MISTAKE THE ABSENCE OF CONFLICT FOR THE PRESENCE OF GOD.

The church doesn't exist merely to do no harm or be a safe place for hurting people (although it's good when we are). We've been given a mission, and we need to take it seriously. Don't mistake the absence of conflict for the presence of God.

Positives 1 through 9: While it's great to be on the healthy side of the line, this status is not without its challenges. The danger comes from the almost invisible yet persistent tendency to grow comfortable or prideful, then stale, then start drifting backward. Any church that fails to keep consciously moving ahead is falling behind.

The New Testament church of Thyatira might have been at +1 or +2. Jesus commended them for their baby steps by reminding them, "I know your deeds, your love and faith, your service and perseverance, and that you are now doing more than you did at first." But they were not strong enough to have rooted out some heresy that had taken a foothold among them (Rev. 2:18–29).

Meanwhile the church at Smyrna might have been at +8 or +9. Despite the persecution and poverty they endured, Jesus told them, "I know your afflictions and your poverty—yet you are rich!" (Rev. 2:8–11).

Positive 10: Well, you're in heaven now. Literally. No church will ever achieve a true Positive 10 until we're gathered with Jesus in paradise. As long as we live in this broken world, even the healthiest church will have room for improvement. But we need to always keep Positive 10 in our hearts and minds as an ideal to strive toward.

NUDGES, NOT LEAPS

If the church you lead or attend is, let's say, at -5, how can it get back into positive territory?

One step at a time.

Your church is probably (almost certainly) not going to jump from a -5 to a +5 in 100 Days. God can do that, and He has on very rare occasions. But you can't program a church to make that jump.

However, you can use principles that can stop the downward slide. Then, once the church has been steadied, those principles can prepare the church to nudge up from -5 to -4 in the following 100 Days.

A CHANGE IN DIRECTION

Sometimes, the change you'll see in 100 Days won't be up the scale, as much as a change in direction. A church at -5 facing uphill in hopefulness is healthier than a church at -5 facing downhill in despair.

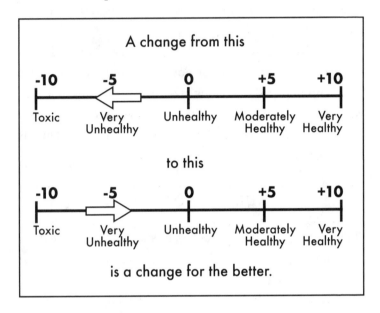

Direction is everything.

PLANNED PAUSES

As you're pursuing healthy change, there will be times when the principles of one week may require more than seven calendar days to accomplish. That's okay. It's better to take a little extra time to handle those challenges well than to hit the somewhat arbitrary deadlines.

But don't let pauses become delays, and don't allow more than one or two pauses over the entire process. If the process takes more than 120–130 days, you'll lose momentum and impact and become far less likely to finish well.

WHAT DOES A HEALTHIER CHURCH LOOK LIKE?

A healthier church is filled with healthier believers—believers who are loving Jesus and each other, who are making disciples, who are cooperating for the advancement of Christ and His kingdom, not for individual agendas.

Unhealthy Churches (-10 to -5)
Aren't obeying the Great Commandment, pursuing the Great Commission, or equipping God's people

Loving, but Ineffective Churches (-4 to 0)
Are obeying the Great Commandment, but not pursuing the Great Commission or equipping God's people

Immature Churches (+1 to +4)
Are obeying the Great Commandment and the Great Commission, but church leaders are overwhelmed and church members are not maturing because leaders are not equipping God's people

Healthy, Effective Churches (+5 and up)
Are doing all three

The best way to determine the health of a church is by how its members are responding to three vital elements: the Great Commandment, the Great Commission, and what I like to call the Pastoral Prime Mandate of equipping God's people to do the work of ministry (Eph. 4:11–12).

The goal of this entire process is to assess where your church is based on those three biblical criteria, then get back on track toward health by reestablishing them. (We'll look at this principle a little deeper on Days 1 and 8.)

INCREASING YOUR CAPACITY FOR EFFECTIVE MINISTRY

Did you notice anything missing in that last section on getting healthier? Like attendance figures?

It's great when a church gets bigger as a result of getting healthier. In fact, it's hard to imagine a healthy church that doesn't want to grow. But getting healthy isn't about numerical growth. It's about striving to increase our capacity for effective ministry no matter what size we are now—or what size we may become.

Bigger isn't the goal. Better is the goal. More effective ministry is always better ministry. As Tim Suttle points out, "The church's job is not to grow. The church's job is not to thrive or even to survive. The church's job is to be the church."[1]

Let's strive to be the church. More effectively today than we were yesterday, then more effectively tomorrow than we were today. That's what getting healthier looks like.

CHAPTER 2

What Can Be Done in 100 Days?

Turning a church from unhealthy to healthy is a daunting task. It starts by working smarter, not harder.

Here's an example.

THE PAINT CAN: A PARABLE

In the 1990s, I led a small group of church members on a missions trip to Bucharest, Romania. The country was just a few years removed from one of the most oppressive, violent, and evil regimes in modern history.

One afternoon we were taking a short break in our hotel. While we were talking, a hotel employee was painting a wardrobe in the hallway—one of those portable closets they use in Europe, like the one in C. S. Lewis's classic book. But there was something about the way he was doing it that was strange.

The employee would brush on a few strokes of paint, disappear into the hotel room for thirty seconds or so, reappear to brush on a few more strokes, then disappear again. This kept repeating. Why?

Then it hit me.

Although the wardrobe was in the hallway, the can of paint was in the middle of the hotel room, so the painter was walking into and across the room for every single dip of paint! But why would he do that? Probably because that's where everything was placed when he arrived. This painter was nearing retirement age, and he had been raised under an extraordinarily repressive regime in which you kept your head down and did the job you were given, no questions asked. Conformity was rewarded, and innovation was frowned upon.

This painter was taking three or four times longer to paint the wardrobe that day because he had been socially, mentally, and emotionally programmed by a corrupt system not to think for himself. It didn't occur to him to perform one simple step that would have made his job exponentially easier, faster, and better: move the can.

What is true of that painter is also true for far too any pastors and other church leaders. Many of us are pastoring under systems that were in place long before us, and it hasn't occurred to us that we can move the paint can.

Like the tired painter in that hotel hallway, it's tempting to leave things where they are right now and keep going through the motions. Turning an entire church around is like getting the entire room ready—far too big a task to even contemplate at the moment.

That's why, for the next 100 Days, we're not going to attempt to overhaul the entire room. We're just going to paint the wardrobe. And the first step in painting the wardrobe is simple.

Move the can.

Make the next step toward health as simple and doable as possible.

What's Your Paint Can?

Like moving the paint can, here are some characteristics to look for when considering what to tackle in the next 100 Days:

1. You can do it right away. The painter didn't need anyone else's help or permission to move the paint can. He just needed the ability to see that it could be done, then do it.

In the church you lead, what fits those criteria? What simple action(s) do you not need permission for? Start there.

2. It will ease your burden, not add to it. Sure, the paint can is heavier than the paint brush, and moving it will be harder than carrying a brush. Once. After that, everything else will get easier.

What tasks can be done in your church that will take a minimal amount of extra effort right now, but will clear a path for several tasks to be done more easily in the future?

3. It will get you to your next step more quickly. After the paint can has been moved, the current task of painting the wardrobe will be a lot easier.

Are there any simple steps you can take to reduce waste and help you get more done with your limited time and resources? Make them a priority.

4. It will be a small first step toward thinking differently. This may be the most important—and difficult—aspect of moving the paint can.

25

It's difficult, because it requires the painter to think differently. But it's important because once you start thinking differently about some initial, simple tasks, you start realizing you can apply the same innovative principles to other harder tasks.

What if you moved the paint can—and *no one* got mad? No emergency committee meetings were called to correct you. The roof didn't fall in. In fact, everything started working just a little smoother. After making a small change once, you'll want to do it again.

Soon, you'll be looking around for other paint cans you can move, other ways to change the long-existing dynamic of systems that have been in place because no one thought to change them for the better.

Now I'm not naïve. I've been in pastoral ministry for almost forty years. I've moved paint cans and been treated as if I were guilty of spitting in the face of our church's beloved founders. So you know what I did in response? I moved the paint can anyway. Then I kept painting.

It's amazing what happens to the naysayers when the wardrobe gets painted in record time, under budget, and with a smoother finish. The complainers either fall away, or they join the paint-can-moving team. And if not? Maybe it's not your wardrobe to paint.

WHY PUT A NUMBER OF DAYS ON GETTING HEALTHIER?

I'm not a big numbers guy. And I've always been more than a little distrustful of books that promise I'll be able to do something in a certain period of time, especially when the "magic" number ends in zero.

So why have I written a book with a number so strongly attached to it?

First, because a number focuses us. It gives us a clear working parameter. Even if we go over the 100-Day mark (which most of us will), the fact that we're on a calendar helps us think more clearly about what needs to be done and when.

Second, the number reveals our priorities. Like when a woman discovers she's pregnant. For the next nine months, family activities and decisions are filtered through the lens of getting ready for the baby. The impending arrival helps us focus so we discover what really matters, what doesn't, what can be delayed, and what can't.

Third, the number gives us a goal. If our church is going to be healthier in 100 Days, we need to decide what aspect of health we're aiming for. Otherwise, we won't know if we've achieved it.

Fourth, the number drives us. You can't hit a goal you haven't set.

Timelines drive us to action. "We want our church to be healthier" is a wonderful idea, but it doesn't inspire action. "We want our church to accomplish this health goal by this date" gets us off the couch.

Fifth, that number invites others to join the team. There's a reason why people who want to lose weight are more likely to do so if they tell others about it (like on social media or in a weight-loss group). When we announce a goal publicly, it's inspirational, exciting, and fun. It attracts people who also want to reach that goal—or want to help you reach it.

It's hard to build a team around an unfocused, unprioritized, uncertain, unclear, unannounced idea. But clear, focused, time-stamped, prioritized goals inspire people to join in, motivate them when the going gets hard, and energize them for that last push to completion.

WHY 100 DAYS?

When something matters, it goes on our calendar.

This is why church attendance matters. If your relationship with Christ matters to you, it's going to affect everything in your life, including your schedule.

It's the same in church leadership—and even more so when the church needs a refresher, a turnaround, or a kick start. If we truly want our church to get healthier, we need a plan. Any plan that's worth something deserves a big spot on our calendar.

When we give a task only half measures, we get half results. But if we give it our full commitment by

- clearing the 100 Days of other distractions
- meeting regularly with the leadership team
- following the daily disciplines together
- giving the process more than 100 Days, if needed
- and surrendering the entire process to Christ in fervent prayer

we'll get the fullest possible results.

There are several reasons for using a 100-Day marker for helping a church get to the next level of health and effectiveness.

First, 100 Days is about how long it takes to assemble and launch something this important. For years, experts have told us that it takes twenty-one days, twenty-eight days, or forty days to establish a habit. It turns out we were off by multiples of at least two or three. According to a peer-reviewed study reported in *Psychology Today*, it takes sixty-six days on average to establish a personal habit.[2]

Second, setting aside an intentional 100 Days makes this big enough to take seriously, but not too big to be intimidating. If I were to tell you that you could make any significant forward motion in your church in forty days, you probably wouldn't believe it. Especially if your church has serious problems. On the other hand, if I told you it would take 365 high-intensity days before you saw even a small step toward health, you'd have a hard time committing to it.

So 100 Days strikes a good balance. It's long enough to have some hope of being effective, but short enough to maintain the necessary intensity to get something done.

Third, 100 Days is about the length of a natural season. Spring, summer, fall, and winter. Each one lasts about ninety-one days. We're created by God to live and effect change according to that timeline.

Fourth, 100 Days can get something going and build momentum for more later. If you

> IT TAKES A LOT OF ENERGY TO GET IT GOING. BUT ONCE IT'S ON ITS WAY, MOMENTUM TAKES OVER.

and your church leaders invest 100 Days into helping your church become healthier, even by a single step, that practice is like starting a freight train. It takes a lot of energy to get it going, but once it's on its way, momentum takes over. Working toward health becomes a habit driven by momentum.

WHAT DO THE 100 DAYS LOOK LIKE?

If you start the 100 Days on a Saturday (which is how this works best), Days 1 and 2 will be a Saturday/Sunday weekend. Then Days 99 and 100 will also be a Saturday/Sunday weekend. This will mean a total of fourteen weeks and fifteen weekends by the time you reach 100 Days.

This span of weeks and weekends is intentional. Starting the 100 Days with an intense, purposeful Saturday meeting, followed by an equally intense, worshipful Sunday, is the best way to hit the ground running. Then, ending with a full Saturday to assess, prepare, and plan for the future, followed by a worshipful celebration on Sunday, is a hopeful way to finalize the process. Everything in this book is written assuming a Saturday start date. If you do it differently, you'll need to adapt for that.

You'll also see that the 100 Days is divided into four main steps:

1. Assess Your Situation
2. Select a Target
3. Train the Team
4. Implement the Plan

The first two steps will get you to Day 50. During that period, you'll rediscover who you are as a church, who you're called to be, and what your first project will be. During the last fifty days, you'll undertake the final two steps, which will pull the team together to actually accomplish your project together.

Within those steps are several intensive Saturday meetings. The meetings will happen every two weeks during the first fifty days with a group we'll be calling the Core Leadership Team (CLT). Then, at the halfway point, you'll assemble Project Teams (PTs), and they will have meetings as determined by their assignments. Also, there's a theme for each week, sermon suggestions for every Sunday, and smaller assignments for every day along the way.

HOW CLOSELY SHOULD
WE FOLLOW THIS PLAN?

No two churches are alike, so no plan can fit every church. But there are some universal principles, and those are what we start with. To get the most out of this process, start by following the book very closely. The first two steps in the front half, especially, are about principles—biblical ones first and practical, methodological ones second. Follow them like a blueprint.

But the further you go, the more each step is open to individual interpretation. Partly because every church is different, but also because Step 1 is designed to help you rediscover God's plan for your church, so it's more important to follow His plan for your church than my ideas for it.

If the book starts out as a blueprint, it ends as a suggestion box—helpful, but not necessarily to be followed to the letter.

CHAPTER 3

Getting to
the Starting Line

If you are a pastor, this 100-Day process will cost you a lot more than 100 Days.

Achieving healthy change is like running a marathon. Marathons are 26.2 miles long, but before runners ever step foot on a starting line, they've run hundreds, even thousands of miles.

For your 100 Days to be successful, it's going to take a lot of prep time. In this chapter, we'll look at what needs to be done before the clock starts on Day 1. Please don't skimp on these steps. If you start without the appropriate preparation, you'll be like the novice who thinks he can run a marathon just by showing up that day. You'll flame out quickly, and you might even sustain some injuries.

If you're not willing to put in the time and effort to undertake the right amount of preparation, you and your church are better off not even attempting the 100 Days. But if you do the prep, while this process can be very challenging, it can also be one of the most exhilarating and rewarding 100 Days of your life and your church's ministry.

So let's get going!

DECIDE ON A STARTING DATE

Timing matters.

If your 100 Days are going to be successful, it's important to choose the right time of the year. Choose a time when you have more than three months with as few calendar interruptions as possible (so the Christmas and Easter seasons are typically not viable).

For most churches, there are four times of the year that seem to meet these needs the best:

1. January through early April
2. Shortly after Easter through the start of summer
3. Through the summer months
4. Through the autumn months

Of the four, January through early April tends to be the best for most churches. Except for Lent, this season of the year has the fewest special days in the church calendar, and it's most likely your Core Leadership Team will have fewer conflicting events than at other times of the year.

ESTABLISH A SABBATH FOR EACH WEEK

This will be an intense 100 Days for the pastor and the CLT. If you go through all 100 without a break it might do more harm than good. So what's the solution?

Sabbath.

Every member of your CLT needs to keep a weekly Sabbath. This rest period is built into the process. Each week will have six days' worth of work to do, not seven.

Sabbath matters for several reasons:

- Sabbath rest is in God's top ten. A Sabbath isn't just a day off, which we might let slip. Sabbath is something we know we should take seriously.
- Sabbath gives our minds and emotions a chance to catch up. Pursuing this process for 100 Days without a break is like running a horse at a gallop without letting it rest, drink, and eat. You'll kill it.
- Sabbath helps us reenergize. If 100 Days seems like a short time to help a church get healthier, it's a long time to work on something this important and difficult without regular breaks.
- Sabbath opens the door for God's surprises. By stepping away we may sometimes see a path forward from an avenue we never would have thought to pursue.
- Sabbath gives you fresh eyes for the next segment. When you come back to the task after your Sabbath, you'll be able to see things more clearly.

Overworked pastors are not healthy, and neither are their churches. Too many pastors are observing no Sabbath at all. For some churches and many pastors, a restoration of Sabbath may bring that step toward health that you need.

CLEAR YOUR CALENDAR

In addition to a weekly Sabbath, it's essential to clear time in your schedule for the extra hours this will cost.

If you're already running at 90 to 100 percent (or more), these 100 Days won't help, they'll hurt—perhaps permanently. Before starting this process, you need to find ways to offload at least ten hours of work from your usual weekly schedule.

What do you normally do as a pastor that someone else can take from you for these 100 Days? Visitation? Weekly Bible study? Administrative duties? If you're bivocational, do you have the ability to reduce your work hours or take some vacation time? Yes, I know what I'm asking. I wouldn't ask if it wasn't necessary. There is simply no way to take on these extra hours—not to mention the extra spiritual and emotional toll—without hurting yourself, if you don't make purposeful space in your schedule.

THE HEALTHY CHURCH LOG

One of the biggest challenges for any church is to figure out how to measure healthfulness. The usual default is to count attendance figures. But the number of church attenders was never the best measure of church health, and it's becoming a less-accurate measure as time goes on.

After all, the church is not called to sell a product, make money, or build a bigger customer base. We're called to love God, love others, and disciple believers who make other disciples. All of those ventures are hard, if not impossible, to measure numerically. This is why this book is *100 Days to a* Heathier *Church*, not *100 Days to a* Bigger *Church*.

> THE CHURCH IS NOT CALLED TO SELL A PRODUCT, MAKE MONEY, OR BUILD A BIGGER CUSTOMER BASE. WE'RE CALLED TO LOVE GOD, LOVE OTHERS, AND DISCIPLE BELIEVERS WHO MAKE OTHER DISCIPLES.

When we come to the part about goal-setting for your 100 Days, I want to encourage you in the strongest way possible not to make that goal numerical.

But if we don't attach numbers to it, how can we know if the church is getting healthier?

Start something I call a *Healthy Church Log*.

A Healthy Church Log is exactly what it sounds like. It's a recorded logbook of anything that happens that is a sign of healthfulness for your church. Write non-numerical signs of health as they happen, or you'll forget them. I recommend this for everyone who is a part of your Core Leadership Team.

So what gets recorded in the log? If someone in the church tells you they shared their faith with a friend for the first time, write that in the log. Was there a couple on the verge of divorce whose relationship was restored into a stronger marriage? Write that down. Was there someone who was resisting necessary change in the church but has decided maybe some changes aren't so bad after all? Write that down.

Obviously, some of the items in this log will be private, but many of them won't be. So give team members a chance to share them with other team members. You may be surprised and encouraged by how many healthy things are actually happening in the church.

ASSEMBLE YOUR CORE
LEADERSHIP TEAM (CLT)

Of all the choices that need to be made before beginning your 100 Days, picking the right people for the Core Leadership Team may be the most important ones. In many churches this first step may also be the hardest one. But putting a team together is essential. In church leadership, as in extreme sports, don't do this alone. Here's why.

My wife, Shelley, went back to college as an adult. While most adults who start back to college flame out without getting a degree (myself included), Shelley not only accomplished her goal, she did it in the designated amount of time. Why? She signed up for a cohort. A cohort is a group of people who start the process together, go through classes with each other, prod each other, help each other, then graduate and walk across the stage to get their diplomas together.

The stats show that Shelley is not an anomaly. Those who attempt to get a later-in-life college degree have a much higher graduation rate when they're in a cohort.[3]

Pastor, you need a cohort, a Core Leadership Team of

willing, passionate, supportive people who will walk through this process with you. After all, a healthy church is not just about you. Without at least a handful of willing participants, this process cannot work and the church will never get healthier.

My friend Dave Jacobs spent years pastoring small churches and now devotes himself to coaching small-church pastors and writing helpful books on small-church ministry. One of his often-repeated axioms is, "Never process anything of significance by yourself."[4] Not only should we not process big issues alone, but we need to get the right people on the team. As Dave also says, "When we're faced with a decision that affects other people and do not include those who will be affected in the decision-making process, those who are affected will feel disregarded and disrespected." Nowhere do those bits of wisdom apply more strongly than in a process of this nature.

So how do we go about assembling a team? The oldest way there is—personal contact. Handpick the people you believe will meet the criteria.

A general invitation isn't likely to get you the people you want, and it may get you some people who won't fit well. But if you go to somebody in the church and say, "You know what? I'm putting together a small team of people because we're going to work on a project to get our church healthier over a 100-day process, and I want you to be a part of that 100 days," the people with passion are going to respond.

So who should you ask? Look for people who are

- Willing
- Available

- Growing in their faith (better to have a two-year believer who is growing than a twenty-year believer who is stagnant)
- Cooperative
- Curious
- Teachable
- Committed to Christ
- Committed to the local church
- Prayerful
- Adaptable
- Reliable

The first time you go through this 100-Day process, it's also helpful for the Core Leadership Team to meet as many of the following requirements as possible:

- Small in size (no more than eight people; three to five members is even better)
- From more than one segment of the church (young and old, official and unofficial leaders, etc.)
- Motivated, but not impatient
- Engaged, but not overly busy
- Softhearted, but thick-skinned
- Honest, but not rude
- Independent, but cooperative
- Solid, but adaptable
- Open to the idea of health and change
- Likely to commit to and last through the entire 100 Days

There are several times in Scripture when leaders are selected to do work for God's people. In each situation, the primary characteristics were never about their skill and experience but about their character and willingness.

For example, Moses's father-in-law, Jethro, told him to appoint leaders "who fear God, trustworthy men who hate dishonest gain" (Ex. 18:21). When the early church chose the seven to oversee the distribution of food to widows, they were to be "full of the Spirit and wisdom" (Acts 6:3). The lists for bishops, elders, and other church leaders include character traits like temperate, sensible, dignified, hospitable (1 Tim. 3:2 RSV), "serious, not double-tongued, not addicted to much wine, not greedy for gain" (1 Tim. 3:8 RSV), and "a lover of goodness, master of himself, upright, holy, and self-controlled" (Titus 1:8 RSV), among many other traits. What they all have in common is that they put character first.

There is no way for me to overemphasize the importance of the team dynamic for your 100 Days. Deciding on the right mix of leaders may take a while, but that's okay. Getting the right people on the team may be the most important decision you will make in this entire process.

Think a lot about it. Pray about it even more. Look outside the group of "usual suspects" for new blood with new ideas. Then give them several weeks, maybe months, of lead time before their schedules align for the marathon ahead.

AN ALTERNATIVE: THE TEST RUN

In many churches, there are rules—written or unwritten—about putting such a team together without proper approval. Especially if the church is in crisis or has a long history of resistance to change, getting approval for your Core Leadership Team may be the hardest step of your process.

If that's the case, here's another option. Do an unofficial test run first. On your first time through the 100 Days, select one or two people who are trustworthy and who will give you some helpful feedback.

In many small churches, the test-run team may consist of the key pastoral staff members, or just the pastor and spouse.

The test run has several advantages.

First, a test run can help you decide whether or not the church is ready for the 100 Days.

Second, the test run helps you see potential issues that can be ironed out before you do the official run-through.

Third, a test run gives you another set of eyes to assess those issues.

Fourth, when you do an official run-through, the test-run team can act as coleaders.

ANOTHER ALTERNATIVE:
THE SELF-SELECTING TEAM

In some cases, especially in smaller churches, the pastor will be asking for trouble by picking the Core Leadership Team himself. If so, one alternative is to make the team self-selecting. The simplest way to do this is to have an open call for those who want to be on the team, then have a meeting in which you lay out the requirements for participating on the team.

Show them the commitment that will be required, the daily assignments, the weekly meetings, and so on. By doing this, those who can't or won't make the commitment will self-select out, and those who want in will know what's required of them. This group should also include a handful of one-on-one pre-meetings with people you want to see on the team. Let them know they're wanted and needed.

This is not an ideal way to select the team, but in many churches this, or some version of it, may be the only way to pull a team together.

The bottom line is this. The stronger the Core Leadership Team, the higher the likelihood of success.

STEP 1

Assess Your Situation

"I will build my church."

Matthew 16:18

CHAPTER 4

Check in with the Church's Owner

Week 1

When I came to Cornerstone as the lead pastor in 1992, the church was in trouble. They'd been through five pastors in the previous ten years. They'd had a church split just over a year before my arrival. The congregation was down to just a handful of very discouraged folks attending on Sunday.

In my interview to become their pastor, the last question they asked was, "What's your vision for our church and our community?"

My answer? "I don't have one."

They looked at me as if to say, "Thanks, but no thanks," but I continued. "I don't have a vision for your church or your community because I've only been here for a couple hours. I don't know you well enough to think I can have those answers. But if I'm called to pastor this church, I'll take whatever time is needed to work with you, listen to you, pray with you, and rediscover

God's vision for this church and the community together."

And that's what we did. It took many steps over many years to get healthy and strong, but it started with that essential decision to do two important things: remind ourselves of why all churches exist and discover the role our specific congregation is called to play in that plan.

START WITH THE ESSENTIALS

Knowing what your church is called to do is an essential starting point for the success of any ministry endeavor.

The main mistake churches make in the revitalization process is to jump right to the specifics of their situation instead of pausing, reflecting, and renewing their understanding of and commitment to Christ and His church. It's essential to take the biblical truths we all (should) know and move them from the background to the foreground.

First, it reminds everyone what the church is really here for. We can get so wrapped up in the immediate needs, frustrations, and challenges of the church that we lose focus on why we have a church to begin with. We can even find ourselves in the position of the church in Ephesus, who lost their first love within less than a generation (Rev. 2:1–7).

It's never wasted time to refocus on Jesus, His mission, and our relationship with Him.

Second, we can never assume that even the most consistent church attenders are truly aware of the mission and calling of the church. We can preach about it regularly and consistently, but that doesn't mean it's registering with the people sitting in the room with us week after week. Simple principles, like the realization that the church exists to honor Christ, not to make us feel comfortable, are often met with incredulous stares, even anger, from people we were convinced knew this already. We can't skip or rush through this essential step.

Rediscovering God's order for the church is the point of this book, starting with this, the first Saturday meeting.

DAY 1 (FIRST BIG SATURDAY)
REMEMBER WHOSE CHURCH IT REALLY IS

Saturday meetings with the Core Leadership Team will be the centerpiece of this process.

This first Saturday is especially important. Not only is it the first day of the 100 Days, but it is the first time the CLT will meet together, and it kicks off the first of your fifteen weekends to-gether. There are five aspects of this meeting to carefully consider.

First, who should be there. Everyone on the CLT must be there—no exceptions. While all absences should be kept at a minimum, there may be one or two absences on subsequent Saturdays. But this starting day is so important that if anyone cannot make it, they need to step off the team. There's simply no way they can catch up if they miss this first day together.

Second, how long to meet. This first Saturday needs to be long enough that the team can spend time thinking, praying, talking, and studying God's Word together. Schedule more time than you think you'll need. What I've seen work best is to set aside 9 am to 3 pm.

Third, the location. Going somewhere away from the church

property is helpful. Subsequent Saturdays can be on the church property, but being in a new setting today can help to inspire fresh thinking.

Fourth, lunch. Plan to eat together. Breaking bread is not just a metaphor for fellowship. It is one of the few behaviors done by all Christians at all times. Whether it's catered, takeout, or potluck (some of my Midwest or Southern friends may call this a covered-dish dinner), having lunch together is a great way to give the mind and body a break, get to know each other better, and talk about something other than the business at hand.

Fifth, the "feel" of the room. Keep it informal and friendly, less like a business meeting or conference and more like a chat in the living room or on the patio. Sit in circles, not rows. Create an environment where people know it's okay to get up and stretch their legs or grab a snack, coffee, or water while the conversation goes on. There will be times when folks will want to use tables for writing and projects, so make sure they're available, but they should not be the main gathering spot.

Before this meeting, assign someone to take notes. Then, after the meeting, have that person collect copies of everyone's pages and consolidate the results into a single document. That document will be reviewed and edited by you so it can be sent to every team member in advance of the devotionals for Week 2.

Now that the logistics are in place, what do you do when everyone is in the room together?

What Does Jesus Want?

Every church should start their assessment not by debating how to change the church, or what new events to do, what new names to give old ideas, or what attendance goals you want to hit, but by considering, "What does Jesus want His church to be?" That will be the entire focus of the first week, but especially of this first day.

Today is not about strategizing new ideas or critiquing old methods. It's about laying all of that aside to focus on Jesus, His church, and His mission.

The biggest challenge of a day like this for most pastors is to strike a balance between dominating the conversation and letting everything devolve into a free-for-all. For the day to be effective, it needs to have a strong leadership hand that allows for all voices to be heard as we listen to Jesus together.

Times of listening to God are different for every church tradition, but Scripture needs to be at the center of it. Here is a practice I have found effective for people who come from a variety of church backgrounds. Before the meeting begins, print up copies of the Church Essentials Conversation Starters from the back of this book. Each page follows a very simple format: 1) a heading, telling you what essential church principle it's about, 2) a set of passages that cover that principle, and 3) plenty of lined space to write down your thoughts and prayers about those passages.

For this first Saturday, I recommend using the first four Church Essentials Conversation Starters, which cover the topics of Church, Worship, Discipleship, and Outreach. There are Conversation Starters available on other subjects that can be done on other days, including Fellowship, Compassion, Leadership, and Prayer. You can find them at KarlVaters.com/100Days.

After a short (fifteen-minute) time of introductions and

prayer, everyone in the room should be in conversation groups of no more than three or four people. If your CLT has fewer than five people total, do this as a single group. Give every person a copy of the first page of Conversation Starters. This page will have a list of Bible passages about the Church and its mission. You'll notice that the text of the passage is not written on the page, just the chapter and verse numbers. This ensures that every group has to look up the passages in a Bible. When we look up the passage for ourselves, it reminds us that we're getting these ideas from God's Word, not ourselves. It also allows people to see the context of the passages, mark their Bibles, and compare translations.

Each conversation group is then given half an hour, from 9:15–9:45 am, to read the passages, talk about what the verses mean to them, and take notes on the conversation. Then take another thirty minutes for each group to share their findings with the entire team, one group at a time. (Both of these half-hour segments will rush by very quickly, so it's helpful to announce the time at ten-minute intervals to move them along.) It's also helpful to have each conversation group start with a different passage so all the passages will get covered.

As each group is sharing what they've discovered from the verses, write those notes where everyone can see, like on a screen, a flip chart, or (my favorite) a long sheet of butcher paper taped to the wall. Pay special attention to ideas that every group has in common (you'll come back to these to remind the team of their common ground) and any "aha" moments that feel new, fresh, and exciting. You can use these as inspiration for new directions. At the end of this conversation, take a fifteen-minute break. Encourage team members to use that break to refresh themselves, go for a walk, ponder, pray, chat, or whatever they need to clear their hearts and minds for the next session. By this time about one-and-a-half hours will have passed, and you'll be ready to start up again, as you can see in the simple layout for the day in the box below.

FIRST SATURDAY CLT MEETING (DAY 1)

9 am: Intro and prayer
9:15–10:15 am: THE CHURCH
    Table conversation: 9:15–9:45 am
    All-CLT conversation: 9:45–10:15 am

10:15 am: Break
10:30–11:30 am: WORSHIP
    Table conversation: 10:30–11 am
    All-CLT conversation: 11–11:30 am

11:30 am: Lunch
12:30–1:30 pm: DISCIPLESHIP
    Table conversation: 12:30–1 pm
    All-CLT conversation: 1–1:30 pm

1:30 pm: Break
1:45–2:45 pm: OUTREACH
    Table conversation: 1:45–2:15 pm
    All-CLT conversation: 2:15–2:45 pm
2:45 pm: Closing comments and prayer
3 pm: Dismiss

After the break, bring everyone together again at 10:30 am. This time ask them to gather in a different group of three to five people. This helps create new relationships, sparks different ideas, and protects the team from falling into old ruts. Hand out the next Conversation Starter (the one on Worship) to everyone and ask them to go through the same process. This discussion time will end at 11:30 am, so your next break will include lunch together.

After lunch, gather the team at 12:30 (again mixing up the groups of three to five) to go through the process two more times using passages that describe Discipleship and Outreach (evangelism). The final session will end at 2:45 pm After a few closing comments, including any relevant instructions about what to do with their papers (they can hand them in or take them after you get copies of them) and what to expect in the coming weeks, pray together and dismiss everyone to go home.

I don't recommend stretching the day any longer. You will have covered a lot of content by 3 pm, which will need time for leaders to internalize and consider. But if you think it would be helpful to cover other subjects including, but not limited to, the ones I've already prepared, a follow-up session with the CLT after church on Sunday (Day 2) or next Saturday (Day 8) is a great option.

PREPARING FOR THE FIRST SUNDAY

Who Knows What, When?

Now we approach another important decision: When do we let the entire congregation know about the 100-Day process?

The answer to that, as you can imagine, is different for every church. There are four options.

1. Before Day 1. The sooner, the better, especially in a relatively healthy church. But even in an unhealthy church, an early announcement is usually the best strategy, since it reduces the likelihood of anyone accusing the church leadership of doing something secretive or shady. An early announcement can also help when you recruit your CLT. It gets people behind you in prayer and starts everyone thinking about eventually serving on a Project Team (coming on Day 43 and following).

2. On Day 2, the first Sunday. For many churches, this will be the ideal day to start communicating this process to church members. Your main weekend service is a natural time to share big plans, communicate the biblical underpinnings of the process, and get people engaged in support of what's happening.

3. On Day 44, the Sunday after the project has been chosen by the CLT. The reason this day is important is because you'll be adding other members into the mix as you create Project Teams (PTs). By the time you start expanding your circle that wide, it will be hard, if not impossible (and probably unnecessary), to keep this from the church body.

4. Never. On very rare occasions, or in very large congregations, a church might walk through this entire process without bringing anyone into it other than those who are leading the change. This happened one time at Cornerstone because several items were in place. First, the changes were relatively small. Second, there was a great deal of trust in the leadership, so most people didn't feel the need to be informed of the inner workings. Third, the types of changes we were making were going to work best if they were subtle and almost subconscious, rather than loud and obvious.

The general rule is to bring people into this process as soon as possible. The last thing you want to do is give people any sense that anyone is hiding anything. That will kill any chance of success. So if in doubt, share more, not less—and sooner, not later. The old rule for leadership was "on a need-to-know basis." The new rule is to assume everyone needs to know, unless there's a clear reason they shouldn't.[5]

Options for Sundays

There are a handful of ways to look at Sundays, depending on the circumstances of your church.

First, if your church's main meeting is on a day other than Sunday, adapt your 100 Days so that the Sunday instructions apply to your regular meeting day. If your main church meeting is on a Saturday night, you may cover Days 1 and 2 in a single day. Or you may want to flip the Saturday/Sunday events to Sunday/Saturday. If your main church meeting is a day other than Saturday or Sunday, feel free to adjust and adapt as needed.

Second, if you need to hold more CLT meetings, you can schedule them on as many Saturdays as you need.

Third, it can be helpful to have a short Sunday lunch meeting with your CLT on the weekends when you don't have a regular Saturday meetup.

For the remainder of this book, we'll operate as though your church's main meeting day is Sunday for the sake of simplicity. Now let's look at how to approach the main Sunday services for these 100 Days.

Getting the Most out of Your Sunday Services

Sunday services are always important for the life of the church. This is especially true during this 100-Day process. During these Sunday services, you will have the chance to set the atmosphere for what's happening, what's coming, and how you'll get there together.

Your sermons and leadership over the next fifteen Sundays, starting with this one, will be directly influenced by the 100-Day process. I won't offer you sermon notes, but I will present occasional ideas. You can use these as prompts or in any way that works for you and your congregation. Preaching is an extraordinarily important and extremely personal practice. No two pastors preach alike, and many churches see the sermon through very different theological lenses. If your church follows a lectionary, feel free to follow your church calendar.

However you do it, be sure to use this chance of the weekly gathering of the congregation to set a tone, communicate important steps, and prepare people's hearts for what is happening.

DAY 2 (THE FIRST SUNDAY)

The first Sunday is an especially important day. It will be your first opportunity to share what's happening with the entire congregation. The emphasis should be to reestablish the foundation of the church, reminding us why we exist and calling us back to that primary identity and purpose.

Today's Big Idea: The church Jesus said He would build. The church you pastor, serve, or attend doesn't belong to you. It doesn't belong to the long-term members, the tithers, the denomination, the pastor, or the lien-holder on the facility. The church—including the local congregation we refer to as "my church"—belongs to Jesus. In fact, every time we use the term *my church,* we need to realize that we're saying "my" in the belonging sense, not the owning sense. In the same way a baseball fan might talk about "my team." It's about commitment and partnership, not possession.

Key Verse: "And I tell you that you are Peter, and on this rock I will build my church, and the gates of Hades will not overcome it" (Matt. 16:18).

Passage of the Day: Matthew 16:13–20

Thoughts to Consider: The first time the word *church* appears in the Bible, it happens as the direct result of a question, not about the mission or vision but about the identity of Jesus. "Who do people say the Son of Man is?" Jesus asked His disciples. Then, after reporting a few of the rumors that were floating around, Jesus asked the all-important question, "Who do *you* say I am?"

Note that the order of the conversation in this passage shows us that Christ's church flows directly out of His character. "Who do you say that I am?" leads very quickly into "I will build my church."

Who is Jesus to you?

Who is Jesus, as seen in the Bible?

How does your picture of Jesus compare to the biblical portrayal of Jesus?

What does this picture of Jesus tell you about what His church should look like?

What might you need to change about your picture of Jesus and His church?

DAY 3 (THE DAILY DEVOTIONALS BEGIN)

This will be the first day of what will be a new experience for many participants—a daily devotional with a specific goal. The idea is to use every one of the 100 Days to build principle upon principle, without overburdening everyone with meetings, but actually using it as a time to slow down, ponder, reflect, and consider where God wants to take His church.

The pattern for the daily devotional is as follows:

- Find a specific time and place to set aside 15–30 minutes.
- Do it as early in the day as possible (if you have to get up earlier than usual, it will be worth it).
- Take a moment to quiet yourself and ask God to speak to you.
- Read Today's Big Idea.
- Read the Key Verse.
- Find and read the Passage of the Day in your Bible (it will put the Key Verse in context).
- Read the Thoughts to Consider about the passage.
- Use a journal to record your thoughts, feelings, and prayers.

Those who have a copy of this book can follow along in it. For those who don't, the daily devotionals can be found for free at KarlVaters.com/100Days.

Since the theme for this week is checking in with the church's owner, the daily devotionals for the next few days will reinforce what we already explored about that subject on Saturday and Sunday.

Today's Big Idea: Consider your motives. We live in a fast-paced world. Some people love that, so they jump on every innovation as soon as it happens, occasionally chasing fads and fleeting styles. Others are more change-resistant. They constantly push back against new things, as though stubbornness were a spiritual gift. That's why it's important at this very early stage to take a heart-check to be sure you're not too far to one extreme or the other.

If you're excited about the possibility of change in your church, ponder why you're excited about it. Is it because this is God's will, or because you love new things? On the other hand, if you're resistant and skeptical about possible changes coming to the congregation you love, is it because the changes truly aren't needed or because you don't like new things, even when they're necessary? The answer for both types of people isn't to keep changing or to keep resisting change but to slow down occasionally and ponder what's happening, why it's happening, and what role God may be calling us to serve in the middle of it. We need to make sure our ideas for the church don't come first, but God's ideas do.

Key Verse: "Who may ascend the mountain of the LORD?

Who may stand in his holy place? The one who has clean hands and a pure heart" (Ps. 24:3–4).

Passage of the Day: Psalm 24

Thoughts to Consider: Psalm 24 establishes that everything belongs to the Lord—the earth and everything in it. When you own something, you get to say what should happen with it. That's why knowing and doing God's will should be the priority of every church and every Christian. Everything is God's. We're the stewards (caretakers) of His possessions, so knowing His will helps us be and do what we were created to be and do.

In the Key Verse, the "mountain of the LORD" and the "holy place" are references to the temple, where God's presence dwelt in the Old Testament era. Clean hands (right actions) and a pure heart (right motivations) are essential for those who want God's presence to be active in their lives—and in their church.

Today we need to consider our motives. What do we want for our church? Why do we want it? Most importantly, do our desires for the church match Christ's desires for His church?

DAY 4

Today's Big Idea: Pondering. Before embarking on anything major in our lives, it's a good idea to slow down and consider what we're doing, why we're doing it, and what the possible results might be. The underlying principle behind this is a seldom-practiced Christian discipline based on an almost-forgotten word: *pondering*.

Key Verse: "But Mary treasured up all these things and pondered them in her heart" (Luke 2:19).

Passage of the Day: Luke 2

Thoughts to Consider: *Hey, isn't this a Christmas passage?* Yes, it is. But it's important for us to detach it from the tinsel, garland, and colored lights and try to read it with fresh eyes. What did it mean to a young (probably teenaged) girl who knew that the baby she had just given birth to was God in flesh and that His life would change the world more than any other life ever lived?

What do you think and feel when you ponder this time of new beginnings for your church? Are you excited? Scared? Worried? Joyful? Concerned? Maybe all of the above? We have to imagine Mary experienced all of those feelings too. But instead of panicking, she took time to ponder them so she could keep moving forward into that frightening, exhilarating, and uncertain future, knowing God's plans were bigger than her deepest fears and greater than her highest hopes.

DAY 5

Today's Big Idea: Repent of wrong attitudes. Attitude is everything. Henry Ford famously said, "Whether you believe you can do a thing or not, you are right."[6] This is true as followers of Jesus, too. If our attitude about the church is not in line with Christ's attitude about His church, everything will go wrong. If our attitude matches Christ's, it will go right. It may not go the way we *think* it will, but that's okay because God's will for His church matters more than our will for our church. Having the right attitude sets the stage for everything that follows.

Key Verse: "Repent, for the kingdom of heaven has come near" (Matt. 3:2).

Passage of the Day: Matthew 3:1–2

Thoughts to Consider: Repentance isn't easy. First, we have to see our need for it. Then, we have to state it to the person whose forgiveness we need. Thankfully, we never need to worry about our repentance being accepted by Jesus.

In today's passage, we see that when John the Baptist was preparing the way for Jesus, repentance was at the center of his message—so much so that he was hated by those who didn't see their need to repent. This is why having a humble attitude and a willingness to confess and repent of our sins is so important. God's will moves forward in repentant hearts.

Are there any attitudes about your congregation you need to reconsider and repent of? Perhaps you've been putting your own will ahead of God's will? Maybe you've been looking at the church through the lens of your personal comfort rather than Christ's commands? Perhaps you're longing for the way your church was in the good old days?

DAY 6

Today's Big Idea: Reconcile, if needed. In your pondering yesterday, did you discover any attitudes that need changing? Maybe some resistance to change? Maybe you've been jealous of a larger or faster-growing church? Don't be too quick to dismiss this possibility. And if you did discover some wrong attitudes, don't beat yourself up over it. We all have them to some degree or another.

Key Verse: "Leave your gift there in front of the altar. First go and be reconciled to them; then come and offer your gift" (Matt. 5:24).

Passage of the Day: Matthew 5:21–26

Thoughts to Consider: No one is perfect in their thought life. Before this process can move ahead, we need to adjust our attitude. Stop what we're doing (leave our gift at the altar), change our attitude (be reconciled with God and others), then proceed with the process (come and offer our gift).

(Note for the pastor: Today is the day to email the notes from last Saturday to everyone on the team, reminding them that we're going to use them during our devotional times next week.)

DAY 7 (SABBATH)

As we saw in chapter 3, every week needs a Sabbath. We'll put it at the end of every week, since that will likely work best for most people, but it can happen on any day of the week that works for your schedule. On this day, there are no specific devotionals to read, no new Big Ideas to ponder. It's time to let go, relax, and do something fun with family or friends.

We do encourage you to spend time in God's Word on every Sabbath day, as always, but on this day it shouldn't be related to the 100-Day process. Just hear what the Lord is saying to you for your life, your family, and your future.

CHAPTER 5

Keeping Christ's Mission at the Center

Week 2

T his book is not about vision-casting; it's about rediscovering a vision that has already been cast. According to Dietrich Bonhoeffer, "God hates visionary dreaming." Those are strong, even extreme words. But they are worth considering. Bonhoeffer went on to say that visionary dreaming "makes the dreamer proud and pretentious. . . . He acts as if he is the creator of the Christian community, as if his dream binds men together."[7]

According to Chase Replogle in his article about Bonhoeffer, "The pastor's first call is not to envision a church but to receive one. We lead by discerning how Christ is forming a community. . . . We are called to a project already underway. . . . True visionary leadership is being first to recognize what God has already formed."[8] But sometimes we forget that. So this week we're going to remind ourselves.

There is a path to health for your church, but it won't be found by trying to follow the latest trend, copying the growing church across town, or going back to a time when your church was vibrant, effective, and filled with people. Trying to become a healthy church by following trends is like trying to win a marathon by riding a bike. A marathon is a footrace of a specific length (26.2 miles) with particular rules about how it must be run (by foot, not with any other mode of transportation). If you want to ride a bike, by all means, ride one. Just don't call it running a marathon.

In any contest, the participants need to understand the agreed-upon goals and rules. You can't win a race if you follow a different set of guidelines from those set up and agreed to. In 2 Timothy 2:5, the apostle Paul tells us that "anyone who competes as an athlete does not receive the victor's crown except by competing according to the rules." Francis Chan reminds us, "God gave us His 'order' for the Church. He told us precisely what He wanted through His commandments in the Bible. In our arrogance, we created something we think works better."[9] Sometimes, the first step in rediscovering Christ's order for His church is to recognize and disassemble what we've put in its place.

> SOMETIMES, THE FIRST STEP IN REDISCOVERING CHRIST'S ORDER FOR HIS CHURCH IS TO RECOGNIZE AND DISASSEMBLE WHAT WE'VE PUT IN ITS PLACE.

DAY 8

To begin today, take a few minutes to review the notes from last Saturday, which were sent or emailed earlier in the week. Reflect on what they mean for you and the church moving forward.

Today's Big Idea: The Great Commandment. Remember the three essential elements to a healthy and effective church: the Great Commandment, the Great Commission, and the Pastoral Prime Mandate ("equipping God's people," from Ephesians 4:11–12). Today we'll look at the Great Commandment, followed by the others over the next two days.

Key Verse: "'Love the Lord your God with all your heart and with all your soul and with all your mind.' This is the first and greatest commandment. And the second is like it: 'Love your neighbor as yourself'" (Matt. 22:37–39).

Passage of the Day: Matthew 22:34–40

Thoughts to Consider: There is no greater, more important section of Scripture for Christians to regularly study, consider, and follow than this passage. In it, Jesus was asked what the greatest commandment was, and He gave a direct answer to that question. There is one God. We need to love God and love those who are made in God's image. That's it.

Then Jesus added an extraordinary statement: "All the Law and the Prophets hang on these two commandments" (Matt. 22:40). In other words, if you're loving God and others, you're doing what God commands. The rest of the Bible is commentary. It's important, essential commentary. It helps us avoid the trap of thinking we can decide for ourselves what loving God and loving others means. But the rest of the Bible is a "how to" that elaborates the two-part command.

When considering the Great Commandment, we need to ask some essential questions. How seriously are we taking Jesus' command to love God and love those who are made in God's image? Is it seen in the practical, everyday life of our congregation? Are there factions in the church? Do people feel loved and cared for? Are new people greeted and welcomed into the fellowship of the church? If not, why not?

DAY 9 (SUNDAY)

Today's Big Idea: The Great Commission. There's only one command of Jesus that's mentioned in all four Gospels and the book of Acts. We call it the Great Commission. It's called that because of how central it is to the life of every believer and any healthy church. Sharing our faith with others isn't an option. It's a command, and it's our joyful commission.

Yet it's easy to get trapped looking inward and forget to look outward. In fact, the more a church is following the Great Commandment, the more tempting it can be to stay in that wonderful, comfortable place of loving God and each other, not wanting anyone else to come in who might disturb the peace. Yet the Great Commandment is exactly the reason the Great Commission matters so much. If we truly love others, we'll want to share the greatest part of our lives with them—even if it makes life a little uncomfortable.

Key Verse: "Go and make disciples of all nations, baptizing them in the name of the Father and of the Son and of the Holy Spirit" (Matt. 28:19).

Passage of the Day: Matthew 28:16–20

Thoughts to Consider: How well are we doing this in our lives and in our church? Are we really sharing our faith? How much of what we do as a church is outward-focused compared to inward? Do people invite their friends to church? If not, why not? And what can we do to change our focus?

DAY 10

Today is the second Monday of our 100 Days. By now, you've been using these daily devotionals for a week. This is a good time to add one more helpful step to this process. Every Monday, take a few moments to scan through what you've already recorded in your notes. This reminds you of the process you're engaged in, and it sets you up for the devotionals to come.

Today's Big Idea: Equipping God's people. The word *pastor* only appears once in the New Testament. In that passage, pastors share the responsibilities of leading the church with those who have four other ministry gifts—apostles, prophets, evangelists, and teachers. And in that passage, all those church leaders are given one task—not to do the ministry for the church but to equip the church to do ministry for each other.

Key Verse: "So Christ himself gave the apostles, the prophets, the evangelists, the pastors and teachers, to equip his people for works of service, so that the body of Christ may be built up" (Eph. 4:11–12).

Passage of the Day: Ephesians 4:11–16

Thoughts to Consider: If equipping God's people for the work of ministry is the primary role of church leaders, it's important to ask ourselves how well we're doing it. Is our congregation consciously and actively engaged in ministry, or is the structure of the church set up so that the pastor and/or staff members are expected to do the ministry for us? Are our church's discipleship programs primarily about attending and learning, or are we engaged in training people to do the ministries of the church?

DAY 11

Today's Big Idea: To seek and to save the lost. If the leadership of the church is called to equip God's people to continue the work of Jesus on earth, what was that work? Thankfully, it's not a mystery we have to dig very deep to figure out. Jesus told us the answer very clearly.

Key Verse: "For the Son of Man came to seek and to save the lost" (Luke 19:10).

Passage of the Day: Luke 19:1–10

Thoughts to Consider: The context of this well-known Scripture is very important. It's the last verse in the story of Jesus meeting Zacchaeus. While this is a favorite story to tell kids, the lessons in it are deep and mature.

Jesus and His disciples were traveling toward Jerusalem, where He knew He would be crucified. By the time they made it to Jericho, less than sixteen miles from Jerusalem (less than twenty-six kilometers), the crowds were so big that Zacchaeus had to climb into a tree to see Jesus. But the tree-climbing isn't the point of the story. After spending time with Jesus, Zacchaeus repented of his sins (which were many) and offered restitution beyond what the law required. Still, that wasn't enough for the religious leaders, who were trying to trap Jesus in the act of doing something against their laws, which is what He did here by eating in the home of Zacchaeus.

Jesus regularly spent time with the wrong people. That was a habit the Pharisees could not abide. So Jesus used opportunities like this one to set them straight. There are no wrong people, but there are broken people, lost people, hurting people. And that's who Jesus came to seek and to save. The religious people of Jesus' day were often confused by Him. And as churchgoers ourselves, most of us have more in common with the Pharisees in Jesus' day than we have with Zacchaeus.

How does Jesus' example of seeking, spending time with, and loving sinners affect us today? What about us? Do we spend any time with the kinds of people Jesus came to seek and to save, or do we spend all our time with other believers? How can we be the light of the world if we only hang out with other candles?

DAY 12

Today's Big Idea: Recommit to the mission. Mission statements are overrated. Most of them remind us of what we plan to do—or *want* to do. But if we're honest with ourselves, most of us—including most churches—don't know what we're going to do until we've already done it. For instance, most great writers don't know what they're going to write until they've written it. Most great lives are lived in the same way. And that's how most great churches happen. We write it, live it, or do it first, then we look back and give it a title—then act like we knew what we were doing all along.

This is not to say that planning doesn't matter. After all, this entire book is based on the value of planning. But the truth is, mission statements don't make great churches. *Doing* the mission makes great churches. The mission is already in place. It's Christ's, not ours. Like a general with troops, or a boss with employees, Christ has assigned tasks so the mission can be accomplished. Very few foot soldiers have anywhere close to a full understanding of what the overall aim of the mission is—they just know what they're supposed to do.

Churches do not become healthy because the pastor comes in with an awesome plan. Churches get healthy when we get in line with God's plan.

Key Verse: "You have left your first love. Therefore remember from where you have fallen, and repent and do the deeds you did at first" (Rev. 2:4–5 NASB).

Passage of the Day: Revelation 2:1–7

Thoughts to Consider: It can be hard to consider a passage from Revelation without getting caught up in endless arguments about eschatology (the study of the end times). But what if we just looked at this passage for what it meant then and there, to the original readers in the church of Ephesus? Since the apostle Paul spent more time there than with any other church, we know as much or more about the Ephesians as any other New Testament congregation. In addition to the book of Acts and the letter to the Ephesians, it gets a significant mention here, as one of the seven churches John sent his letter to.

Yet as strong as the foundation of the Ephesian church was, within less than a generation they were already forgetting what they were built on. They'd left their first love. If this can happen so quickly to the church in Ephesus, it can happen to us. We, like them, can easily forget what should be motivating us and become consumed by our own agendas. Because of this, we must constantly remind ourselves of the essential truths of the church, including asking some important questions as we pursue church health:

"What are my motives for wanting a healthier church?"

"Is it just one step toward getting bigger?"

"Is my pride a factor in this?"

"Am I competing with another pastor, another church, or my own expectations?"

"Could I be okay with a healthier church, even if it didn't result in numerical increase for our congregation?"

"Is this about my ego or God's glory?"

No one but Jesus has completely pure motives. But we should at least acknowledge as many unhealthy motivations as we can, then do our best to reduce them.

DAY 13

Today's Big Idea: What will you sacrifice for the mission?
Anything of value will cost us something. The greater the value, the higher the cost. So while it's one thing to make a commitment, it's something else entirely to make a sacrifice for it.

Church events are worth committing to. In fact, if our faith doesn't at least get us to commit something from our schedule on a regular basis, we'd have to question the level of our commitment. But sacrifice? Is there a church event or program we'd willingly make a significant sacrifice for?

Probably not.

Hopefully not.

While commitments can be made for important things, sacrifice is reserved for truly essential and eternally valuable things. So today as we study the value of offering ourselves as sacrifices, we need to establish two important principles: First, this is not a sacrifice for salvation. Jesus has done that once and for all. There is nothing we can do and nothing we need to do to earn our salvation. It is a gift from God (so no one can boast). Second, this sacrifice is being offered to Christ and His church, not to your local congregation, pastor, denomination, or theological constructs. Those are important, to be sure. They're worth committing to, and they will be the arena where our sacrifice plays itself out. But only Jesus and His church are worth truly taking up our crosses in sacrifice for.

Key Verse: "Therefore, I urge you, brothers and sisters, in view of God's mercy, to offer your bodies as a living sacrifice, holy and pleasing to God—this is your true and proper worship" (Rom. 12:1).

Passage of the Day: Romans 12:1–8

Thoughts to Consider: While many people say they'd die for Jesus, this passage is telling us we need to live for Jesus, offering not just our thoughts or spirits to Jesus, but our bodies—not necessarily to die for Jesus (although we should be willing to do so, and many have and are still called to do that) but to live for Him. Commitments cost us something. A sacrifice costs us everything.

What does it mean to offer our bodies as a living sacrifice? How does that relate to Jesus' command to take up your cross? Does it ever seem like it might be harder to live for Jesus than it might be to die for Him? If so, why? If not, why not?

Finally, what would you be willing to sacrifice for Christ and His mission? Be specific. Look especially at ideas, events, comforts, and ways of thinking that you have grown accustomed to that you might need to give up or change.

DAY 14 (SABBATH)

CHAPTER 6

The Culture Conversation

Week 3

According to Max De Pree, "The first responsibility of a leader is to define reality. The last is to say thank you. In between the two, the leader must become a servant and a debtor."[10] That is the pattern we're following during these 100 Days. That first responsibility—defining reality—is what we're concentrating on for these starting weeks. Then, from Days 50–98, we'll act as servants and debtors, working hard and recognizing that we owe everything to Jesus. Finally, on Days 99 and 100, we'll celebrate and say, "Thank You!"

Defining reality must always be our starting place—not casting a vision, not assembling a team, not making a plan. A wise leader begins by making an accurate assessment of what is actually taking place, right here and right now, then sharing that reality with the team.

So far, we've worked together to define Christ's reality for

His church. This week, we'll start taking a hard, honest, but necessary look at how well our specific congregation is living up to that standard. What are our strengths? Our weaknesses? Our resources? Our needs? Without an honest accounting of our current situation, we'll never be able to get where we're going.

This is not easy. We're all susceptible to self-deception. Some see the world through rose-colored glasses, always convinced that our circumstances are better than they actually are. These are the optimists. (If that's you, hang on to that attitude. We'll need you when things get hard.) Others see the world as worse than it is. They're the skeptics. If there are ninety-nine events going well, they'll see the one incident that's not quite up to snuff. (If that's you, hang on to that. We'll need you at times when we're ready to jump straight in without a plan.)

Right now, we need the die-hard skeptics to come out from behind your impenetrable fortress, and we need the eternal optimists to remove those rosy shades. Let's dare to see our church and ourselves as we truly are.

There's a reason this reality check is happening in Week 3, not Week 1. By now, your attitude and expectations about the church should be somewhat different from two weeks ago. Instead of relying on our feelings about *our* church, we've spent some serious time considering God's will for *His* church.

We tend to make one of two big mistakes about our feelings. On the one hand, we give them too much credit, filtering all of reality through them. On the other hand, we can discount our feelings as though they don't matter at all. Neither of these extremes is healthy. Instead, we need to start with a desire to know and do God's will first. Then He can use our feelings as one of the tools to do His will. After all, God created us to have emotions, so they must have a purpose in His plan.

This week, we'll take a look at what we're feeling, thinking, and learning about our church's current condition, bringing those thoughts and feelings under submission to Jesus.

DAY 15
(SECOND BIG SATURDAY CLT MEETING)
CONSIDER THE CHURCH'S CULTURE

This is a big day. We'll be taking a look at the condition of the congregation using three diagnostic tools. It's possible we won't like what we find, but the more challenging this process gets, the more important it is to be accurate about it. We can't get better any other way.

Like the first Saturday meeting, we will start at 9 am with purposeful, passionate prayer. Do not shortcut this vital step. Give the day to the Lord, especially a day as challenging and pivotal as this one. How important is prayer to a day like today, not to mention this entire process? Thom S. Rainer tells us, "I have never seen a successful and sustaining change take place in a church without prayer. Never. Not once."[11]

Then, ask your team members how they've been doing with their Sabbath-keeping and daily devotionals. This should be an honest, open time of sharing successes, failures, concerns, frustrations, and shared experiences. Those who are having a hard time keeping up with their daily devotionals or fully observing a restful Sabbath should not be shamed but encouraged.

SECOND SATURDAY CLT MEETING (DAY 15)

9 am: Intro and prayer
9:15–10:45 am: The Church Culture Talk
    "What kind of soil are we?" 9:15–9:45 am
    Conversation: 9:45–10:15 am
    The Soil Rating Score: 10:15–10:30 am

10:45 am: Break
10:45–11:30 am: How Severe Is Our Culture Issue?
    Poll the team: 10:45–11 am
    The Mission/Culture conversation: 11–11:30 am

11:30 am: Lunch
12:30–1:30 pm: The Life Cycle of a Church
    Teaching the Life Cycle: 12:30–1 pm
    The Life Cycle conversation: 1–1:30 pm

1:30 pm: Break
1:45–2:45 pm: What's Your Current Stage?
    X marks the spot: 1:45–2:15 pm
    Putting it all together: 2:15–2:45 pm
2:45 pm: Closing comments and prayer
3 pm: Dismiss

As you can see in the schedule, sessions will be divided into two equal parts, before lunch and after lunch. The morning will consist of the Church Culture Talk. After lunch we'll be looking at the Life Cycle of a Church. The goal of the day is not to find solutions or decide on a project. It's to discover where the congregation is right now.

Morning: The Church Culture Talk

Every church has a culture—an unwritten, often unrecognized set of rules that governs everything the congregation does. "That's how we do things here" is a statement about your church's culture.

It is impossible to overstate the importance of a church's culture. In His parable of the sower (Matt. 13:1–23), Jesus describes four types of culture, or soil, that a Christian or a church body can have. (I owe a big debt to Jim Powell and his book, *Dirt Matters,*[12] for introducing me to this lens.)

1. The path/hard soil: This represents a church that has grown hard and stubborn. Good ideas don't penetrate, new methods are instantly rejected. This stubbornness can be the result of legalism, hurt, anger, habits, or ignorance. It's tempting to think that all stubborn churches need is to be shaken out of their slumber, but in my experience, the root of most stubborn churches isn't sinfulness, it's pain. Many churches have grown hard as a way to protect themselves. In fact, if a church has been hurt by a lack of integrity from leadership they will often withdraw into themselves for protection, like a turtle pulling into its shell.

2. Rocky, shallow soil: This soil represents a church that doesn't reject good ideas outright. They usually smile, nod, and seem to approve easily, but there's no follow-through. They're not deliberately rejecting anything, but they don't have the discipline to prepare or practice, show up on time, or engage fully when they're there. After the event or service is over, they may rush to their cars, or if they stick around, they chat with their friends, ignoring first-time guests and failing to lift a finger to help in cleanup or teardown.

3. Thorny, busy soil: This soil indicates a church that, like the second soil, doesn't reject good ideas immediately, but instead of lacking in maturity, they're too busy to give a new idea the attention it deserves. This is especially the case for a church that has lost a lot of members in recent years. If the church used to be bigger, you may still have all the programs from when the church was big enough for them. The membership has shrunk, and the church's ability to support those programs has faded, but the programs are still there, taking up space. Like clutter in a home, clutter can build in a church—and it can wreak havoc on the physical building, our emotional capacity, and our calendars.

4. The good soil: This soil represents a church in which the culture is soft, deep, and cleared of clutter. Church members are ready for change, excited about the future, prepared to get to work, and unencumbered by excess activities.

What's Our Church's Culture?

After walking everyone through the four types of culture, ask team members to take a few minutes to write down their thoughts, as they answer the following question:

"How would you rate the four soils numerically?" This will give you your church's Soil Rating Score.

After that's been done, tally up everyone's scores. The soil type with the highest aggregate score indicates how your key

---

The Soil Rating Score
Rate each soil from 5 (very) to 0 (not at all) for your church at this current time.

Our church culture is:

	5 (very)	4	3	2	1	0 (not at all)
Stubborn	☐	☐	☐	☐	☐	☐
Shallow	☐	☐	☐	☐	☐	☐
Busy	☐	☐	☐	☐	☐	☐
Healthy	☐	☐	☐	☐	☐	☐

---

leaders see your church right now. The one with the lowest is the least like your church. If more than one soil receives a very high score, you will have more than one issue to deal with.

After tallying the scores, take a short break, then gather the group and start the second phase of the culture assessment. "How severe is our church's culture issue?"

How Severe Is Our Culture Issue?

If the fourth soil (a healthy church) is your highest number, *congratulations!* This will be a relatively easy day, and your 100 Days has a high likelihood of success. But if your assessment reveals that any other soil is your highest score, this part of the conversation will be challenging, even difficult, but very important. Given that you're reading this book, we'll proceed under the assumption that your church is struggling to overcome a culture represented by one of the first three soils.

Take another poll of the group. This time ask them to rate the severity of the culture issue from one to five on the Severity Score. There's no zero option this time, since we're rating something that has already been shown to be an issue:

The Severity Score

Our church's culture problem is:

☐ 5—Extremely severe (not fixable?)

☐ 4—Severe (possibly fixable)

☐ 3—Fairly severe (probably fixable)

☐ 2—Serious but not severe (fixable)

☐ 1—Not serious at all (easily fixable)

Here's an example of how it might work. If your church's highest Soil Rating is Stubborn, ask the group how severely stubborn they believe the church to be. Then ask them to give *just this characteristic* a Severity Score number.

If more than one characteristic is tied or almost tied for highest score, then rate both of them. For instance, if Stubborn and Busy got a 3.9 and 4.0 on the Soil Rating Score, ask everyone to rate the church's severity on each of those characteristics. Doing this can help clarify how severe one or the other is, bringing you closer to an understanding of where your greatest need might be. If Stubborn gets a 4.8 average Severity Score, while Busy gets a 3.0, then Stubbornness will be your biggest issue to tackle.

Now you have a much more accurate picture of what your CLT thinks about the church's culture.

Should We Tackle Mission or Culture First?

This leads to the final question of the morning. After presenting the Severity Score to your leaders, ask them, "Should the main goal of our 100 Days be changing the church's culture, or launching a new mission, vision, or idea?" This may be the most important question of the entire 100-Day process. It will be addressed in more detail later (on Day 43), but it's important to start the conversation now.

If you have determined that your church's culture is any of the first three soils and you've assessed that the problem has a Severity Score of 3 or higher you must, must, *must* deal with that culture issue first.

I cannot overstate the importance of this.

You have to stop throwing good seed on bad soil. Fix the culture first.

The good news is, this 100-Day process can help you change the culture just as readily as it can help you launch a new mission or ministry idea. If you have the will to commit to it, church culture can change. I've seen it happen. I've led unhealthy churches through this to a big culture change. It won't be easy (I've said that already, haven't I?), but it can be done.

But first, lunch. Because everything looks better after a good meal.

Afternoon: The Life Cycle of a Church

Almost anything can be plotted on a bell curve—extremes on the edges, the bulk in the middle—including a human's earthly life span, with birth on one end, death on the other end, and the bulk of life lived in the big bulge in the middle. It's the same with the life of a congregation. But, unlike a person, a church's earthly life span doesn't have to be limited to seventy or eighty years on earth. If we pay attention to the church and to God's working within it, congregations can constantly renew themselves.

We need to start with an understanding of a church's life cycle and where our congregation is on it. To do this, I've designed a bell curve that will help us see the Life Cycle of a Church. This is not a new idea. I've borrowed pieces of it from many other places,[13] but the final design is one we've used at Cornerstone many times. Here's what it looks like:

Moving from left to right, a church is in birth stage when it is planted. For your church that could be years, decades, or centuries ago. At the Birth stage, everything is exciting and scary. Your church planting team is fully committed. You work long hours, but you're truly like a family, facing new experiences together.

After a while (usually a couple of years), the church moves from the Birth stage into a time of Growth & Learning. The growth may or may not be numerical, but it certainly will be experiential. You've tried a few things because "it seemed like a good idea at the time" only to find that some of these ventures weren't such a great idea after all. So you keep what works and toss what doesn't, but along the way you learn a lot and grow from those experiences.

That leads inevitably to a season of Experience. You're still learning and growing, but now most of your decisions are based less on "Let's see what works" and more on "This worked, so let's do it again" and "That didn't work, so let's not try that anymore." In this stage, your decisions are based more on experience than experimentation.

After the Experience stage comes what is usually the longest season of a church's life: Maturity. For many congregation members, this feels like what they've been aiming for all along. We're here. We've arrived. We're at the top of the mountain. But what tends to happen to people after they arrive at a destination? They stop traveling, that's what. Because of this, Maturity is often one of the most dangerous stages of a church's Life Cycle. While all seems strong and stable, momentum is slowly being replaced by inertia. What makes this so dangerous is that, unlike problems that were obvious in previous stages, the perils of this stage are comfortable and therefore mostly invisible.

If a church stays in the Maturity stage too long, it inevitably leads to the next stage, which is the first negative stage of the church's life: Stubbornness.

In the Stubbornness stage, years of hard work to plant,

grow, and reach maturity have taken their toll. The church has started to attract more settlers than pioneers. Having a stable budget, owning land, and getting comfortable with a set style of worship can be very comforting, then far too comfortable. Soon church members don't just enjoy their comfort zone, they insist on it. A church that used to thrive on innovation and risk now does everything they can to minimize innovation and risk, sometimes even seeing change or risk-taking as enemies. From this stage on, the longer it takes a church to recognize their downward slide and do what's needed to correct it, the further down the bell curve they will slide.

If a church has spent a long time in Maturity, or has had an unusual amount of success, this Stubbornness stage can last a very long time. As long as the money keeps coming in, the bills are paid, the people's felt needs are being met, and no one rocks the boat, this can last for years—even decades. So why not stay here? Because churches that stay in Stubbornness don't stay on mission, and no church that gets off mission can last long—no matter how much land, how much money, or how many members they have accumulated.

Stubbornness eventually leads to Pain & Loss. The shift is usually felt first in a reduction in passion, then a loss of members (through transfer and/or death as the congregation ages), then a drop in finances as givers start departing. Yes, that's the new paradigm. It used to be that people stopped giving first, but the new reality is that the money is often the last indicator to drop. Shockingly, according to Tony Morgan of The Unstuck Group, "Per-capita giving can actually be the highest when the church is in decline."[14] Unfortunately, it often takes that final monetary hit before a lot of declining churches start noticing—or at least start caring—about their predicament. At this point, conversations become more about "the good old days" than the future, and about maintaining what we have more than reaching out to bless others.

While it's hard to see the need for a turnaround at Maturity, and hard to accomplish a turnaround at Stubbornness, it's almost impossible the deeper a church goes into Pain & Loss. In fact, at this stage, it's far easier and often highly recommended that a church chooses its own time and manner of closure, using the opportunity to give its remaining material assets to another ministry that's on the left side of the bell curve rather than seeing all their resources slip away into acrimony, debt, irrelevance, and death.

It's sad to see a church close as they reach the Death stage. It's especially sad when the warning signs were there, usually for years, and the death of a congregation could have been avoided. That's the reason I wrote this book. To give churches at all stages a fighting chance to start a new cycle of life, hope, and health.

A Practical Note to Pastors

Pastors, when teaching this Life Cycle to your Core Leadership Team, I highly recommend making the visual aspect of it as big and clear as possible. What we do at Cornerstone is take a roll of butcher paper about ten to twelve feet wide and put it along the wall, then use thick markers to draw the bell curve and add each stage in big block letters as we walk through it with them. We like to sit the team members at a table (or tables) covered with butcher paper as well, then encourage the team members to draw the illustration on their table as it goes along.

In recent years several studies have shown that writing on paper is a huge aid both to memory and to sparking creativity. When we write on paper, the synapses in our brain that spark memory and creativity get lit up like a fireworks show.[15]

Where Are We on the Life Cycle?

After walking through this bell curve with the team, pose the next question. Namely, where do you think our church is on this curve? Write that question in big letters on the butcher paper wall, and make sure they write it on their tables, too.

But before they answer that question, walk them through one last piece of information. There's an interesting and significant correlation between the stages on the up (left) side and the stages on the down (right) side. As seen in this diagram, each stage on the positive side has a shadow on the negative side.

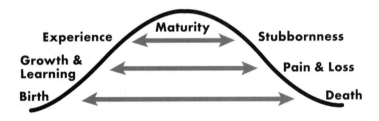

First, a church can believe they're in a place of Experience when, in fact, they're in the Stubbornness stage. After all, Stubbornness is brought on by an overreliance on our Experience, instead of remaining open to new ideas. Be careful not to confuse the two. Second, Growth & Learning can often feel like Pain & Loss. It's hard to grow, and it's even harder to learn something new. This is often one of the reasons people resist it. Finally, Birth can feel strangely similar to Death. Both involve radical change. A church that's going through a rebirth may be getting rid of assets, making radical changes to their format, and so on. Because the changes are so severe and the desire to restart is so strong, we can deceive ourselves into thinking the last gasping stages of a dying church are the first (also gasping) stages of life.

Why Does This Matter?

You may be wondering why we're calling this a cycle. After all, a cycle is usually illustrated by a circle, not a bell curve. Well, here's the good news . Instead of declining and then dying, a church can catch itself before it dies and start a renewal process all over again, thus becoming a cycle.

When that happens at its optimum level (Maturity), it looks like this:

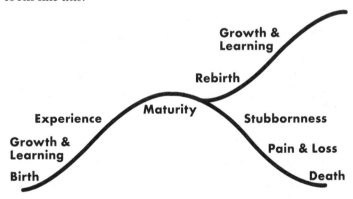

Unfortunately, very few churches are aware enough or pro-active enough to hit the renewal button at this optimum time.

When a church is in Maturity and the leaders are presented with the idea that now might be a time to consider a Rebirth, most of them will understandably react with confusion, even anger. Why would a church voluntarily go through the painful process of renewal just as we're at the greatest time of our church's life? Why not just stay at Maturity? The reason is simple, but profound. It's stubborn to want to stay in the Maturity stage, and Stubbornness is the first step on the downside of the bell curve.

The reality is that very few churches whose leaders are grabbing for a book about how to make their churches healthy are likely to be in the Maturity stage. And churches in the Birth, Growth & Learning, and Experience stages haven't reached a need for rebirth. So most of you are likely to be at some spot on the down (right) side of the bell curve. But what stage?

What's Your Current Stage?

As we've done twice before, it's time to take the temperature of the room. This time it's "X marks the spot." Literally.

Ask each person to take another look at the bell curve on their table, then use a marker to make an X on the spot where they think the church is right now. There are no right or wrong answers at this point. This is about their feelings right now. Then take all of the responses and transfer them to your bell curve on the wall in front of everyone.

If all the X's are in one general spot, you have one more piece of the puzzle. If one or two people have put an X in a significantly different spot from the rest of the group, start a conversation with them about why they chose it. Don't criticize them. They're not wrong. They may have information others don't have. The goal of this conversation is to gain information, not to force agreement. In some instances, the outliers may be misunderstanding what their stage is. Others may have questions themselves about why everyone else saw it differently. It's worth taking the time to have this conversation. If the outliers come around to seeing it everyone else's way, great! If not, maybe they're seeing what others are missing. The plan should be to act going forward based on the majority opinion but be open to the idea that this may need to change as new information comes in that might prove the outliers right.

But what if the X's are all over the place and there is little or no agreement at all about where the church is? The likelihood is that the more pessimistic people in the room are probably right. If the core leaders of a church can't even agree on what stage of decline you're in, you're probably worse off than most people are acknowledging.

This is still not a reason to panic. While it may feel disheartening, this too is helpful information. If the team can't get on the same page, getting the leaders to agree on the church's current condition might be the issue that needs fixing. Doing that in what's left of the next 100 Days will get the church healthier.

After this, take another short break, then come back for the final stage of what has been a long, challenging, but hopefully informative day.

Putting It All Together

And now we come to the final event of this, your second Saturday as a CLT—putting it all together using the -10 to +10

Healthy Church Continuum (from chapter 1). Here it is again:

Draw this on your wall and have the team members draw it on their tables. Now your team will put all of the day's information together to give you an idea of where you are on this continuum.

Start with where the day began. Remind everyone of what kind of soil the church has (your Soil Rating result) and write it down on the wall, using the Our Church by the Numbers guide. This will determine if your church is on the left (-) side of the continuum (for Stubborn, Shallow, or Busy soil) or the right (+) side (Healthy soil). But don't mark a place on the continuum yet. You're only narrowing it down right now.

Then write down your church's Severity Score. If your Soil Rating is 4 or higher, you're on the outside edge of that side (8–10), if it's in the 3s, you're in the middle (3–7), and if your Severity Score is in the 2s or under, you're close to the center (0–2). Finally, where is the church on the Life Cycle bell curve? When you put those three elements together, does it show health or lack of health? If it shows health, you're on the right side of the continuum. If lack of health, you're on the left side.

Then look at how strong the numbers are. Are you slightly, moderately, or severely on one side or the other? If slightly, you're close to the zero center line on your side of the continuum. If moderate, you're nearer a -5 or +5. If severe, you're on one end or the other.

OUR CHURCH BY THE NUMBERS

Our **Soil Rating** showed our church culture to be:

_____

This puts our church on the ☐ Left (–) ☐ Right (+) side of the **Healthy Church Continuum**

☐ Stubborn   ☐ Shallow   ☐ Busy   ☐ Healthy

The **Severity Score** for our church's culture is:

_____

This puts our church on the ☐ Outside Edge ☐ Middle ☐ Inside (near zero) of that side

Our number on the **Healthy Church Continuum** is:

_____

Our **Life Cycle** placement is:

_____

This will make our 100-Day challenge   ☐ Very Doable
☐ Challenging   ☐ Very Difficult

After considering these possibilities, ask the members for one last opinion for the day. Another X marks the spot. Have each member draw an X on their table where they think the church is currently, then transfer all the answers to the wall. Then walk through the same process of conversation as you did for agreement/disagreement on the bell curve. If the group is in full agreement, you know where you are and where you're headed. If you have some disagreement, talk it through. If you're in complete disagreement, this is yet another sign that you may be worse off than previously thought.

Now What?

So far, you've spent two weeks rediscovering what the Bible says about *the* church and one long day starting to understand where your current congregational culture is. For a lot of churches, this will feel like a very low point. But that's okay. This moment is very similar to the first time someone attends an Alcoholics Anonymous meeting and says the fateful words, "Hi, I'm Terry, and I'm an alcoholic." It may feel like the lowest point of Terry's life, but that admission is actually the starting line back toward health and wholeness.

Going forward, you have a much better idea of where your church really is. You've been brought to the point of saying, "Hi, we're First Church, and we're in Pain & Loss," or "We're Community Chapel, and we're Very Unhealthy."

This may feel horrible. But remember, you're only beginning to define your reality. You don't have the whole picture yet, just one aspect of it. This is the first step, not the entire race. Over the next two weeks, we'll add much more information—details about your strengths, your hopes, and your assets and resources. When it all comes together you'll have a baseline from which to work.

This is why *100 Days to a Healthier Church* doesn't start with checking out cool, new church trends, deciding whether or not to hire a new staff member, or figuring out how to fix Sunday school. Moving toward health always requires something much deeper than that.

For the next six days we're going to unpack what we've seen today, then for the following week we'll start to engage with possible solutions so we can find a way forward. The first step in that? The Sunday service.

DAY 16 (SUNDAY)

Today's Big Idea: Is our culture ready for the mission? If you're using your Sunday sermons to help the congregation walk through this process, I'd suggest a sermon for this Sunday of "Digging through the Dirt" on the parable of the sower.

Jesus describes a farmer sowing seed that inexplicably lands on four different types of soil. I say "inexplicably" because every person listening to Jesus that day lived in an agrarian society. Even those who weren't farmers by profession lived close enough to the land that they were aware that no farmer just randomly scattered seed. They all knew to prepare the soil properly and place the seed in holes that had been dug for them.

Because Jesus started His parable with this twist, every listener immediately would've thought, "This isn't about farming. It's about something else entirely." It's the same in our churches.

After years of doing things "the way we've always done them," it's easy for a church to stop being about the mission and start becoming about something else entirely.

This Sunday is a great time to remind the church body what we're supposed to be about. A sermon on the truths of the parable of the sower is an ideal place to start. Use the text and the lessons learned from the Saturday meeting to prepare the hearts of the people for the changes that are coming. If the church is Stubborn, don't beat them up for it. Offer them the chance to start softening their hearts. If the church is Shallow, help them start the move toward maturity by reminding them that church exists to worship Jesus and serve others, not to make ourselves comfortable. If the church is Busy, don't attack their beloved programs and events. Give them some *what ifs* to think about.

What if we focused in on a few things we did well?

What if we stopped scattering seed randomly and started placing it carefully on good soil?

What if we could transfer our valuable time, energy, and resources from things of lesser value to things of greater value?

Today is not the day to berate people for their faults, but to give them hope for the future. After all, your CLT may be coming to church today feeling anywhere from excited about new possibilities to terrified and discouraged about the size of the problems. Yesterday was about assessment. Make today about encouragement.

Key Verse: "But the seed falling on good soil refers to someone who hears the word and understands it. This is the one who produces a crop, yielding a hundred, sixty or thirty times what was sown" (Matt. 13:23).

Passage of the Day: Matthew 13:1–23

Thoughts to Consider: How did our church culture get to where we are now? Have I contributed to that in any way? What will it take for our church to make the necessary changes? How can I contribute to it becoming healthier?

DAY 17

Today's Big Idea: Remember how you felt on Day 1. At this point in the process, it's possible to fall into the trap of assessing the church as though it's something detached from you. It's so easy to think, "The problem with the church is . . . " or "The pastor should be doing more of . . . " or "I hope that person is paying attention to . . ." The big problem with such feelings is that they're pointed in the wrong direction—outwardly not inwardly. The church is not out there, it's in here. It's not them, it's us. It's me. The sooner we can recognize that, the sooner real, healthy change can take place.

Today's exercise is to think back a few weeks to how you felt and what you thought about your church before this entire process began. I know, it seems like this should have been done on Day 1, or even earlier. But if we had taken too much time to consider our feelings before considering God's will, it would have been hard, if not impossible, for our feelings not to become our priority. Again.

Instead, now that we've framed everything through the lens of God's will, let's take some time to think back and remember what you felt and thought about the church and your role in it. Were you

Hopeful?
Confused?
Enthused?
Depressed?
Cautious?
Motivated?
Overworked?
Uninspired?
Inspired?
Or something else entirely?

In considering your previous thoughts and feelings, don't just select words from this list. It's only there to provide a few examples. Take a few minutes to remember how you felt. To prompt your memory, consider: What did you say in private conversations about the church? What was your understanding about the church's past? Your feelings about its present state? Your expectations for its future? How did you react when you were asked to serve on the Core Leadership Team?

Write those ideas down. Make a list, write in full paragraphs, use bullet points, whatever works for you. The format doesn't matter. This list is yours. No one else will ever see it unless you choose to show it to them.

Key Verse: "Remember that you were slaves in Egypt and that the Lord your God brought you out of there with a mighty hand and an outstretched arm. Therefore the Lord your God has commanded you to observe the Sabbath day" (Deut. 5:15).

Passage of the Day: Deuteronomy 5

Thoughts to Consider: After God brought the Hebrews out

of slavery, He met with Moses to give him the Ten Commandments. One of those commandments was to take a Sabbathday rest. Imagine how that felt to people who had spent four hundred years in slavery, when one of God's top ten rules was "Take a day off!" But note that in the explanation for this command, God tells them that one of the ways to use that day was to remember where they had come from—specifically, to remember their former slavery. This command is repeated regularly throughout the Old Testament, but this is the first time, and it came just a few months after their release from bondage.

God knew they needed to remember where they had been so they could appreciate where they were going. This is why we need to take a few moments doing the same thing right now: remembering where we were. Even if it doesn't feel like we're free yet (the Hebrews were a long way from the promised land at this point), it's never too early to remember where we're coming from.

DAY 18

Today's Big Idea: Record how your feelings and expectations are changing. Take a look at what you wrote down yesterday about how you felt before this process started. Then look at your notes from the conversation you had about church culture on Saturday. How different are they?

For most people, there will be at least a few significant differences. Take a few moments to reflect on those differences and what that reveals about how your feelings and expectations about the church are changing.

Key Verse: "Let us consider how we may spur one another on toward love and good deeds" (Heb. 10:24).

Passage of the Day: Hebrews 10:22–25

Thoughts to Consider: How have your feelings about your church changed in the last two weeks? How do you expect them to change? How do you hope they'll change? How do you need them to change?

DAY 19

Today's Big Idea: Consider what you may need to change. Yesterday you reflected on how your feelings about the church are changing. Today you go deeper. In addition to your feelings about the church, it's important to look at how those feelings have resulted in actions and what the consequences of those actions have been. What role have you played in creating the church's current culture? Were you enforcing a bad culture without realizing it? If so, what might you be called to do to help change it?

Key Verse: "God, have mercy on me, a sinner" (Luke 18:13).

Passage of the Day: Luke 18:9–14

Thoughts to Consider: The story of the Pharisee and the tax collector is a tricky passage. Every time we read it, it feels like one of those "Gotcha!" moments. We want to sit in quiet judgment of the Pharisee, but the moment we do that, we start thinking, "I'm glad I'm not like that Pharisee" and we prove how much of a Pharisee we really are.

So let's pay attention to the tax collector instead. As much as everyone hates paying taxes, the Roman system of taxation and collection was so much worse than we can imagine. Like Zacchaeus from Day 11, this man's job consisted of cheating people, selling out his own countrymen, and enriching himself to support an oppressive regime. But something had happened to him. He had come to an awareness of his sin and arrived at the temple to repent. He knew he needed to change, and his repentance was accepted by God.

What do we need to change? Have we been willing participants in creating an unhealthy culture in our congregation? We need to be careful here, because if we think we haven't, we might find ourselves to be more like the Pharisee than we'd like to admit.

DAY 20

Today's Big Idea: Commit yourself to be open to what Jesus is doing. Right now, you may have an idea about where you think these 100 Days will take your church. Maybe you have a few possible outcomes in mind. "It will probably be A, but if something else happens, it will be B, and if that goes sideways, we might end up at C." But any time we give God an A, B, or C choice, He always picks D or M or 7 or purple. God often takes us somewhere completely off our scale of possibilities.

> MATURE BELIEVERS DON'T ASK GOD TO FOLLOW OUR PLANS. WE COMMIT TO FOLLOWING GOD'S PLANS.

We need to be ready, willing, and committed to follow Jesus wherever He takes us—however expected, unexpected, surprising, or seemingly mundane.

Key Verse: "Commit to the LORD whatever you do, and he will establish your plans" (Prov. 16:3).

Passage of the Day: Proverbs 16:1–8

Thoughts to Consider: Take note that in the Key Verse, God doesn't *follow* our plans, He *establishes* them. They become our plans, but they start as His plans, not ours. Mature believers don't ask God to follow our plans. We commit to following God's plans.

DAY 21 (SABBATH)

CHAPTER 7

The Culture Shift

Week 4

DAY 22 (SATURDAY)

Today's Big Idea: Addressing the culture issue. For a week now, we've been considering the culture (the soil) of the church. Now we start the process of asking, *What will it take to change that culture from unhealthy to healthy?* For the next week, in advance of our next Saturday CLT meeting, we will start writing down our thoughts about what needs to be changed, how serious that need is, and what initial steps might lead us there.

Knowing whether your church culture is Stubborn, Shallow, or Busy matters because each problem requires a different approach.

A Stubborn culture (the dirt on the hardened path) is impenetrable. You won't soften the hearts of a Stubborn church by beating people up. That will just harden them even more. Instead we need to recognize that dirt gets hard because pressure has been applied to it over a long period of time. In the case of Jesus' parable, the hardened dirt is a pathway. It's not a road, which is a planned hardening for purposes of travel. It's a path. Paths happen when people walk over them constantly. That must be how the most hardened members of your church feel—walked on.

Most Stubborn churches don't get there because people wake up one day and decide to be mean and unmoving. They typically get there from years of abuse or neglect. They used to be an active part of the field, ready for planting and harvest, but after being walked on by one difficult circumstance after another, they've grown hard. They've subconsciously decided they won't let anyone hurt them again. That's what their hardness usually is—a protective layer to keep them from being hurt again. So they don't need to be treated harshly (as much as you may want to react sternly). Gently, softly, like a gentle rain on hard soil, their hearts need to be softened. The number-one way to get there is to earn their trust again.

A Shallow culture is soft on the surface, but only on the surface. There's no depth or maturity. The members of a Shallow culture say *yes* to great ideas with their mouths, but there's very little follow-through in their actions. The answer for a Shallow culture is depth and maturity. A Shallow church needs to go deeper in understanding what God's Word tells us about how we as a church should behave. The exercise from our first Saturday together when we discussed Bible passages about the purpose of the church is a great place to start.

Be careful here. It's tempting to think that what Shallow churches need is better teaching, but many Shallow churches

FOR A STUBBORN CULTURE

Key Verse: "I will give you a new heart and put a new spirit in you; I will remove from you your heart of stone and give you a heart of flesh" (Ezek. 36:26).

Passage of the Day: Ezekiel 36:24–28

Thoughts to Consider: What hurts caused our Stubbornness? How severe are those hurts? What will it take to start softening hearts and earning trust?

FOR A SHALLOW CULTURE

Key Verse: "Do not merely listen to the word, and so deceive yourselves. Do what it says" (James 1:22).

Passage of the Day: James 1:22–27

Thoughts to Consider: What caused our church culture to be Shallow? How severe is this problem? What will it take to start getting people to step up and follow through?

FOR A BUSY CULTURE

Key Verse: "Come to me, all you who are weary and burdened, and I will give you rest" (Matt. 11:28).

Passage of the Day: Matthew 11:28–30

Thoughts to Consider: What caused our church culture to be so Busy? How severe is the division of labor between those who are too Busy and those who are passive? What will it take to reduce activity and work smarter?

are led by great preachers. What makes them Shallow, to reuse an old but appropriate cliché, isn't that they don't know what to do, but they don't *do* what they *know*.

A Busy culture is soft, maybe even deep, but they're ineffective because they're trying to do too much. Usually a handful of leaders are overwhelmed with busyness, while the rest sit, watch, and consume what's being done for them. The enemy in this scenario (the thorns) isn't the church members—not even the Busy ones. It's the calendar. There are too many events on the schedule.

When you live in a Busy culture, it's easy to think that the way forward is to implement an exciting new event, program, or activity. This must be firmly resisted. The solution for a Busy culture won't be found in what we add but what we remove.

Today's verses and thoughts are divided into three buckets. Don't attempt all three (although you Busy folks might be tempted to). Pick the one that's needed for your church's culture.

DAY 23 (SUNDAY)

Today's Big Idea: Toward a better culture. After relating the parable of the sower, Jesus directly explained its meaning. This gives us a great opportunity to revisit the parable after identifying the challenges last Sunday. It's important to teach about all four types of soil. First, because that's where the passage takes us. Second, because no church faces just one of those issues to the exclusion of the others. Third, because these three culture issues interact with each other—like threads in a fabric, when you pull one, you affect the others. Finally, the focus shouldn't be on the problems but on the solution: helping the culture become softer, simpler, and deeper.

Key Verse: "But the seed falling on good soil refers to someone who hears the word and understands it. This is the one who produces a crop, yielding a hundred, sixty or thirty times what was sown" (Matt. 13:23).

Passage of the Day: Matthew 13:18–23

Thoughts to Consider: How can we help our church start making the needed shift in culture? Is there anything I need to change in my actions or attitudes that can contribute to a better culture?

DAY 24

Today's Big Idea: Avoiding false answers. Now that we've identified the soil and considered renewing it, we need to take an important look at misunderstandings that often exist about each soil.

If your church has a Stubbornness problem, many church members might fear that if the church soil becomes soft, it will become compromised. But the solution to Stubbornness isn't compromise, it's adaptability. That's what softness allows for— the ability to receive good seed and adapt to the crop that the seed wants to grow in us. The goal is to transform the soil from hard to healthy. Healthy soil doesn't make us more susceptible to the thorns of false teaching and bad attitudes. Healthy soil recognizes and rejects thorns as it recognizes and receives good seed.

Likewise, the antidote to Shallowness isn't more teaching, it's greater effectiveness. That's true depth. When a farmer softens the soil, it's not to go as deep as possible, it's to make the soil ready to receive the seed and produce a harvest. It's about being active in the harvest. It's not depth for the sake of depth, it's depth for the sake of effectiveness.

Finally, the flip side of Busyness isn't laziness, it's simplicity. In fact, Busyness and laziness often go hand in hand. One group in the church gets overbusy, so another group sits back and lets them do all the work. Other times laziness leads to a last-minute frantic rush. However it happens, laziness and busyness are not opposites, they're coconspirators. The solution is simplicity and efficiency.

Key Verse: "Are you so foolish? After beginning by means of the Spirit, are you now trying to finish by means of the flesh?" (Gal. 3:3).

Passage of the Day: Galatians 3:1–3

Thoughts to Consider: The churches in the region of Galatia started well, then got sidetracked. So the good news is, the problems in your church are nothing new. The early church had them, too. In Galatia, they started with faith but traded for the false solution of works-based religion (what the apostle Paul called "the flesh").

What parallels to Galatia might exist in your congregation? Have you been trying to solve faith problems with works-based solutions? Is there a better way to approach this than what you've been doing? How does your personal attitude need adjustment to a better mode of thinking?

DAY 25

There is never a one-size-fits-all solution for real-life problems. The church with a Stubborn culture needs a different solution than the church with a Shallow or Busy culture. And even if two churches have a Shallow culture, their solutions will be different because the Shallowness was caused by different circumstances.

However, there are some universal, underlying principles. As we saw yesterday, a Stubborn church needs to become softer and more adaptable. A Shallow church needs to go deeper and become more effective. A Busy church needs to reduce clutter and simplify. So depending on where your church is right now, consider how each of these principles might apply in your situation. Over the next three days, we will look at these solutions one at a time. But don't skip any days just because that day's topic doesn't address your church's main culture issue. Each culture issue affects how we approach the other culture issues.

Today's Big Idea: Softer and more adaptable. When I arrived at Cornerstone, they'd had five pastors in the previous ten years. Every time I tried to launch something new, the congregation resisted. Not because they were hostile but because they'd been hurt. Remember how soft soil can become a hardened path after it's been walked on? That's what happened to the good folks in our church.

Since the church members were hurting, we didn't push back against them. Instead we loosened the ground by re-earning their trust. Day after day, week after week, year after year, we spent time in fellowship, discipleship, worship, and hopefulness. We kept our promises. Like parched ground responding to a long, steady rain, it softened their hearts, fed their spirits, and earned their trust.

Key Verse: "As he was scattering the seed, some fell along the path, and the birds came and ate it up" (Matt. 13:4).

Passage of the Day: Matthew 13:1–23

Thoughts to Consider: What helped our church become softer and more adaptable will be different from what it will take your church to do the same thing. But almost always, the core of the solution is earning back trust, and there's only one way to accomplish that: do the right thing, every time, for a long time.

Is there anything you've done that has damaged people's trust? Or, as in my situation, are you paying for someone else's mistakes? Either way, what can you do to start earning trust again? Are you willing to stick around long enough to see soft ground return?

DAY 26

Today's Big Idea: Deeper and more effective. What do you do when everyone in church is in agreement, but no one follows up on anything? I pastored a church like that once. They were great folks—loving, kind, and enthusiastic. But they hadn't been equipped to do the work of ministry, so they had no depth. New ideas were met with eagerness, but the congregation expected it all to be done for them instead of pitching in.

Shallow soil needs to become deeper. This happens

through relationship, teaching, and worship, but mostly it happens through equipping. As long as the pastor or a handful of church leaders does everything for everyone, they'll let you. So the leadership needs to start creating an environment in which people are trained, equipped, assigned duties, followed up, and sent out again.

Key Verse: "Some fell on rocky places, where it did not have much soil. It sprang up quickly, because the soil was shallow" (Matt. 13:5).

Passage of the Day: Matthew 13:1–23

Thoughts to Consider: It's easy to mislabel equipping as delegating. But you can't delegate a task to someone who hasn't been equipped. So if you've had previous frustrations trying to get people in the church to step up and help out (maybe even in this 100-Day process), it may be that you've been delegating tasks to people who haven't been equipped to do them. They may not be as unwilling as they are untrained.

Ask yourself what you might have done to contribute to a culture of Shallowness in your church. Are you doing things for people, instead of equipping them to do it? Are you spending more time alone in tasks than with a team? Are you burning out good people because they get as overworked as you are?

If any of this applies to you and your church, consider seriously what steps you need to take to shift the way ministry is done. We'll get into some details about how to do this in Week 12 with an in-depth look at how Jesus mentored seventy-two of his closest followers, but today it's important to honestly assess where you and the church are currently.

DAY 27

Today's Big Idea: Reduce clutter and simplify. It's easy to think of a Busy church as a healthy one. After all, activity means life. But there's a big difference between active and hectic. The most effective people, leaders, and churches are active, but they're never hectic. When you're hectic, someone else is in charge of your life and schedule—and it's not who you want in charge.

Like houses, churches don't have to work at getting cluttered. Clutter just happens—to the facility and the schedule. Meetings get added, but nothing gets dropped. Outdated events keep reappearing on the calendar. No matter how hard you work, there's always more to do.

Key Verse: "Other seed fell among thorns, which grew up and choked the plants" (Matt. 13:7).

Passage of the Day: Matthew 13:1–23

Thoughts to Consider: Effective churches aren't driven by events, programs, or schedules. They're driven by the mission. And the mission is simple: Love Jesus, love others, share your faith, and disciple believers. There are a couple of simple but essential questions every church must ask on a regular basis if they want to avoid clutter. What do we do well that we'd like to do more of? And what do we do poorly that we'd like to do less of?

As you consider what to write down, don't think about what you want to do, what a church consultant told you to do, or what another church in town might be doing. Look at your current situation. This is not about wanting or wishing;

it's about knowing your strengths and weaknesses. (These lists will be used, along with everyone else's lists from today, at your next Saturday CLT meeting. But they're conversation starters, not demands.)

What do we do well?	What do we do poorly?
_____	_____
_____	_____
_____	_____
_____	_____
_____	_____
_____	_____
_____	_____
_____	_____

DAY 28 (SABBATH)

STEP 2

Select a Target

*"Now strengthen
my hands."*

Nehemiah 6:9

CHAPTER 8

Consider Your Options

Week 5

DAY 29 (THE THIRD BIG SATURDAY)

A church does not become healthier by doing a project. But the right project, at the right time, for the right reasons can be a wonderful rallying point. Even though a church's concerns must always be focused on the internal and eternal, Thom S. Rainer has noted, "Your church will not be ready for change until it experiences some action steps of an outward focus. This outward focus prepares members for change."[16] A visible project can narrow your focus, give you a sense of urgency, and create a sense of community.

But projects are not necessarily events. As we'll see in more detail when we get to the Decision Day in two weeks (Day 43), your project can initiate a change in direction, a change in attitude, or a change in methodology.

Today's Big Idea: Brainstorm project ideas. By now you're familiar with the pattern for the Big Saturday meetings. As much as we're shaking everything up, it's helpful to come back to this familiar pattern to help us think, pray, talk, and strategize together.

In today's sessions we're going to look at four essential questions about what our church currently does.

What?
What if?
Why?
Who?

This will help us get everything on the table for a possible project. By the end of the day, we'll have them categorized in a way that will help us make sense of what we're currently doing so we can develop a framework to help us narrow our options. It's helpful to think about the next two weeks like a funnel. Today we're at the top of the funnel. It's wide and inclusive. We're putting everything in. There are no bad ideas. We'll leave nothing out. We won't start narrowing the funnel until next week. Simply put, this week we go wide; next week we'll go narrow.

First Session: What?

We begin again with prayer—not as a cursory introduction (because that's what church people do, right?) but as the necessary starting point for everything. Then check in with the group by asking a few questions like "How's your Sabbath-keeping been going?" "What have the daily devotionals been teaching you?" and "Is there anything you need help in as we move forward?" Again, if anyone is falling behind on their devotionals or struggling to keep their Sabbath day, don't pile on the guilt. Offer prayer, encouragement, and any help you can give.

As on previous Saturdays, if you have more than six people on your CLT, gather everyone in groups of three to five, and focus everyone's attention on the screen, whiteboard, flip chart or a stretch of fresh butcher paper on the wall. The butcher paper is the format I'll be assuming as we move forward.

In the middle of the butcher paper, write the heading *What Does Our Church Do?* Then ask everyone to start pitching in. Literally, what do we do? As each event, idea, program, and concept is mentioned, write it in the center of the butcher paper, leaving plenty of empty space on the sides (you'll see why soon).

Do you do a weekend worship service? Write it down.

More than one? Write down each one individually (as in, "9 am worship," "11 am worship").

Ushers? Write it down.

Missions giving? Write it down.

Full-time or part-time pastor? Write it down.

There's no event, program, ministry, or idea too small or obscure to list. Don't forget seasonal or annual events, background tasks (like setup and janitors), and cultural emphases (traditional or contemporary worship style). Write down everything the church does. In most churches, the list will be much, much bigger than expected.

After you have everything written down on the wall, ask

everyone to grab a small piece of paper. After they've taken a few minutes to consider the big list, they should use that paper to write down the three to five items they personally think the church does best, followed by the three to five items the church does least well. They're not to list the items they like or the ministries or activities they think the church *should* do. Write

---

THIRD SATURDAY CLT MEETING (DAY 29)

9 am: Intro and prayer
9:15–10:45 am: WHAT?
    List everything the church does: 9:15–9:45 am
    Table assessment: 9:45–10 am
    All-group assessment: 10–10:45 am

10:45 am: Break
11 am–12 pm: WHAT IF?
    Table discussion: 11–11:30 am
    All-group discussion: 11:30 am –12 pm

12 pm: Lunch
1–2 pm: WHY?
    All-group discussion

2 pm: Break
2:15–2:45 pm: WHO?
    All-group discussion
2:45 pm: Closing comments and prayer
3 pm: Dismiss

---

down what the church does well right now and what you do poorly right now. This is a great time to refer to the lists everyone worked on from Day 27.

After everyone has written those down, have someone at each table collect everyone's answers and report all the answers from their table to the rest of the room. Every time an item gets a "What we do best" mention, put a check mark next to that item on the wall. Every time an item is on the "What we do poorly" list, give it an X.

Once all the check marks and X's have been assigned, make two columns on the butcher paper, using the blank spaces on the sides. Every item that received a check mark will be written in the left column, with the item that received the greatest number of check marks on the top, down to the item with the fewest checks on the bottom. After that, do the same on the right side of the wall with the items that received X's. But this time put the items with the fewest X's on the top, the most X's on the bottom. What you will end up with is a visual representation of what your CLT believes to be your church's greatest strengths and biggest weaknesses, as you move top left to the bottom right.

Label the columns this way:
Do More? (left)
Keep as Is? (middle)
Do Less? (right)

The end result should look something like this:

DO MORE?	KEEP AS IS?	DO LESS?
11 AM WORSHIP PARENTING CLASSES HOSPITAL VISITS PASTORAL COUNSELING MISSIONS GIVING	FOOD BANK　VBS　9 AM WORSHIP xxx xx KIDS' NIGHT xxxx　JANITORIAL　11 AM WORSHIP ✓✓✓✓✓✓✓✓✓ YOUTH GROUP　SUNDAY SCHOOL　CHOIR PARENTING ✓✓ CLASSES ✓✓✓✓　MIDWEEK PRAYER STAND & GREET xxxxxxxx USHERS　MEMBERSHIP CLASS　ANNOUNCEMENTS PREACHING　HOSPITAL VISITS ✓✓✓✓　GIVING MISSIONS GIVING ✓✓　PASTORAL COUNSELING ✓✓✓✓✓ BULLETIN　DEACON BOARD　RECOVERY GROUP WORSHIP TEAM　WEEKLY SMALL GROUPS xxxxxxxxx　FELLOWSHIP DINNERS BIBLE STUDY　FUNERAL SERVICES SENIOR MINISTRY CHRISTMAS EVE　RIDES FOR SENIORS EASTER EGG HUNT	VBS 9 AM WORSHIP KIDS' NIGHT STAND & GREET WEEKLY SMALL GROUPS

Once it's done, everyone should take a photo of it. You'll need it later.

Now it's time for a short break.

Second Session: What If?

After the break, bring everyone back to the tables, but in different groups. Ask each table to consider what's written on the butcher paper as they discuss the following "What if?" questions:

- What would happen if we put more time, effort, prayer, and resources into the items in the column on the left?

- What if we did less of—or stopped doing—items in the column on the right?
- What if we were able to take the time, energy, and resources we're currently pouring into items we don't do well (the right side) and put them into items we do well (the left side)?

In this exercise, it's easy to fall into a couple of traps. First, be careful not to oversell the importance of items on the "Do Less" list on the right side. Even if something seems indispensable, it may not be. For instance, one of the items that many smaller churches don't do well might be "retain a full-time pastor." This happens in a lot of churches. Some churches are chronically without a pastor, others are constantly changing pastors, and many are only able to afford the salary for a bivocational pastor. Many churches see this as a problem that *must* be fixed. But is it? The truth is, there have always been healthy churches that function without the full-time paid pastor role we've become accustomed to, from the New Testament church until the present. It may be time for some churches to let go of this expectation and take a step toward health either by realizing that a bivocational pastor is not a problem (paging the apostle Paul!) or by figuring out how to share the leadership of the church without paid clergy.

The same can be said for the church building, musicians, and other aspects of church life many of us take for granted. Outside of a handful of essentials, like gathering regularly to worship Jesus, receiving Communion, praying, and learning the Scriptures, very little of what we think we need is actually required for a vibrant, healthy church body.

The second trap is not to downplay what your church does well (the left column). For instance, there's a tiny church in Kurtz, Indiana. Several years ago when I was there, I was surprised to see a thriving church in such a remote, low-populated area. When I asked the pastor how the church remained so vibrant in such a remote place, he told me an amazing story.

Several years ago, while sitting at yet another funeral reception, this pastor wondered why God had called him to a (literally) dying church in a dying community. *All we do well,* he thought, *is funeral receptions.* Then it hit him. *We do this well!* So the pastor went to the funeral director and made him a promise. Whenever anyone in this town dies, their church would give the grieving family a funeral reception for free so that family would have one less worry on such a hard day. As a result, that church has been able to bless their community, and their church has become a rallying point for the people of that region because they recognized and leveraged a strength that most would have considered a weakness.

When something like funeral receptions lands on the list of things your church does well, it's easy to dismiss. But what if, like the good folks of Kurtz, Indiana, you leaned into it instead of away from it? What if something you think of as a weakness is actually a strength? This is why it's important to consider absolutely everything you do. You may find an unrecognized strength hiding in plain sight.

After thirty minutes of table discussion about these "What

if?" questions, once again have a spokesperson from each table report their results to the entire group. Write bullet points from these conversations on whatever space is left on the butcher paper, and make sure someone is assigned to take more detailed notes you can refer to later.

You will now be more than ready to break for lunch.

Third Session: Why?

After lunch, we're going to take the information we've already gathered and ask the all-important question, "Why?"

Several years ago I was participating in a Q&A session after speaking at a church leadership conference. One of the first questions asked was, "How do we fix Sunday school?" It's a reasonable question, and it was asked out of a difficult place. But I didn't answer it directly. Instead, I encouraged the inquirer to go a little deeper.

"Let me ask you a different question first," I proposed. "Why does your church have Sunday school?"

"Because we need to raise up the next generation to love Jesus and know Scripture."

That's a great answer. So I responded with, "Then that's the question we need to ask. Not 'How do we fix Sunday school?' but 'How do we raise up the next generation to love Jesus and know Scripture?' If Sunday school is the best way to do that, then let's fix Sunday school. If not, find something that works better."

That's what this "Why?" session is all about. Reframing our questions so we can get to better answers. For this, we won't be breaking into groups. Instead, bring everyone together and present them with some "Why?" questions to get everyone thinking differently.

Gather at the wall again, and consider the items on the left, in the "Do More" column. This time, instead of asking what we do well or poorly, start with the top item and ask, "Why do we do this particular item?"

As people answer that question, take note of how closely their answers do or don't fit with Christ's mission. Is the correlation obvious and positive? If not, ask another "Why?" question. "If this item isn't essential to Christ's mission, why are we doing it?" Sure, we may do it well, but there's no sense being good at something that isn't central to God's call on our church, is there? As D. L. Moody famously said, "Our greatest fear should not be of failure, but of succeeding at something that doesn't really matter."[17]

If any items on the "Do More" list don't stand up well to the "Why?" questions, feel free to move them to the "Do Less" column.

Then take the process over to the items in the column on the right. Ask, "Why are we doing those?" If the answer isn't obvious, it's confirmation that they need to stay there. But if the answer is "That's something we absolutely need to be doing better at, because it's essential to the church's mission," maybe it needs to be moved from the "Do Less" column to the "Do More" column.

Be careful not to let your personal preferences cloud your judgment. While it's possible but unlikely that an item needs to move from left to right, the likelihood that an item needs to move from right to left is infinitesimal. So why bother looking at them this way? Because the practice of thinking like this can help clarify our priorities. These conversations are a big reason why we spent so much time in the first few weeks reestablishing our understanding of Jesus' plan for His church. We must get better at filtering everything we do through the lens of Christ and His mission, not our personal preference.

Finally, take a few minutes to ask "Why?" about the items in the middle. If anything stands out as a huge oversight, and the general consensus is that it needs to be moved to one of the other lists, do so. But don't spend too much time there. The other columns will already be giving you more than enough to consider.

After a short break, come back for one last session to wrap up this long, but hopefully fruitful, day.

Fourth Session: Who?

So far we've taken note of virtually everything our church does, what we do well, and why we do it.

But as we saw at the start of the day, we're still at the top of the funnel. We're putting everything into the mix and categorizing it in a way that helps us think more clearly about it.

So how do we move forward from here? How do we decide what to do first? And how do we turn that into a doable project that will help our church become healthier? Those answers won't be coming today. Instead, those are the questions everyone needs to go home with.

Over the next two weeks, we're going to use our daily devotionals to help us see these items through a biblical filter. As the funnel narrows, this filter will help us decide what to keep and what to lose. So far, all we've done is note our strengths and weaknesses and ask some questions about them. On our next Big Saturday, in two weeks, we'll be ready to pick a project.

In this final, short session, we'll set the table for the next two weeks by walking through today's devotional together.

Key Verse: "Now to each one the manifestation of the Spirit is given for the common good" (1 Cor. 12:7).

Passage of the Day: 1 Corinthians 12:1–11

Thoughts to Consider: No work of God goes forward on great ideas alone. It requires people—people who are passionate, people who work together, people who love the cause, people who are called by God to make a difference.

Those people have been given gifts from the Holy Spirit—gifts that aren't meant to be kept to themselves. According to today's Key Verse and Passage of the Day, the gifts of the Holy Spirit are clearly meant to be used for the sake of the assembled church ("the common good").

As your day together concludes, take some time to consider this great truth. As big as the church's challenges may seem right now, our God is bigger, the mission is Christ's, and He has put all the pieces in place that are needed to move His church forward.

Instead of closing out the day by contemplating the size of the task or trying to make sense of all the information we put on the table, take a few moments to remind everyone that the success or failure of this task does not rest on our shoulders. First, there's an entire congregation to draw on in order to do what needs to be done. Second, don't forget it's Jesus' church, so the burden rests on Him. Finally, no matter the size of your congregation, be it 1,000, 100, or 10 people, God has distributed His gifts to His people to serve His church. In other words, every church has all they need to do what Jesus wants them to do.

So, during the coming week, don't think about tasks, projects, events, programs, or a timeline. Lay them aside for now. We'll come back to them. Instead, take the week to think, pray, consider, and ask God's guidance regarding people. Ask Him to open your mind and heart to see the people God has called to this church, the people who are yet to show up, the people you may be reaching as you move forward, and, within a couple of weeks' time, the people you'll be adding to your team.

As you close in prayer together, ask God to help you keep your eyes open to see gifts you never saw before, in people you may never have considered before, to accomplish a mission you never thought was possible before.

(Note for the pastor: It's always a good idea to save your butcher paper as a reference point, or at least take a photo of it. But the one you filled out today needs to be kept close. You'll be pulling it out again on Day 43.)

DAY 30 (SUNDAY)

Today's Big Idea: Love and the spiritual gifts. Now that we've addressed what we do and why we do it, it's time to start looking at the tools available to help us tackle the issues the church faces—starting with the greatest resource any church has, the human resource, under the guidance and power of God's Spirit.

Today we're looking at the spiritual gifts. Unfortunately, this topic has often been a huge point of theological contention. Different theological traditions have vastly different understandings about what the gifts are, who is called to operate in specific gifts, which gifts are still in use, even how many gifts there are. Regrettably, these debates have stirred up a lot of anger, dissension, and conflict in the church, which, ironically but not coincidentally, is exactly the opposite of what the spiritual gifts are designed to do.

When we spend too much time debating the gifts, we get confused, divided, and neutralized. This is why I say this dissension is ironic, but not coincidental. When a church body operates under the gifts of the Spirit, we're engaging in a spiritual battle, and that battle has an enemy who wants to short-circuit our effectiveness whenever possible. So if our attention can be turned from using the gifts to debating and fighting over them, the enemy wins. But when we're able to stop debating the gifts and start using them, our mission becomes clear, our hearts are united, and our impact is increased exponentially.

This week we will not be engaging in debates. I have no interest in changing or challenging your church's understanding of the spiritual gifts. I just want to see them used for the blessing of the church, so the church can be a blessing to its community and the world.

Key Verse: "If I have the gift of prophecy and can fathom all mysteries and all knowledge, and if I have a faith that can move mountains, but do not have love, I am nothing" (1 Cor. 13:2).

Passage of the Day: 1 Corinthians 12–14

Thoughts to Consider: Wait a minute! I thought we were looking at the spiritual gifts today! Isn't the Key Verse from the Love Chapter? Yes, it is. The Love Chapter happens to be right in the middle of the longest teaching passage about spiritual gifts in the entire Bible. It's there for a reason—not as a step away from the spiritual gifts, but as an essential, central part of them.

In the Key Verse the apostle Paul reminds us that even if we're utilizing the spiritual gifts to such a degree that miracles are occurring as a result, if we're not acting in love, they (and we) are nothing. That is why this chapter is purposefully written right in the middle of some very thorough, even harsh teaching about the spiritual gifts—as a constant reminder for all churches at all times that the gifts must be used in a spirit of love toward one another.

The spiritual gifts are powerful. Because of that, they can bring great blessing or cause great damage. To bring great blessing, they have to be used with proper understanding and the right attitude—and that attitude is love. Love doesn't weaken the gifts; it turbocharges them, coordinates them, and releases them for a torrent of blessing on the church and the community that church ministers to.

> LOVE DOESN'T WEAKEN THE GIFTS; IT TURBOCHARGES THEM.

DAY 31

Today's Big Idea: What are the spiritual gifts? There are three New Testament passages where multiple spiritual gifts are mentioned: Ephesians 4, Romans 12, and the passage we'll be looking at today, 1 Corinthians 12–14.

Paul's instructions to the Corinthian church contain the longest, most thorough teaching about the spiritual gifts in the New Testament. In them, we read about their proper functions and value, while also coming to a better understanding of how they can be abused if we're not careful to use them well.

How many spiritual gifts are there? It turns out the answer isn't as simple as the question. Lists of spiritual gifts vary among faith traditions from as few as seven to as many as twenty-seven. In the sidebar on page 135 you'll see a list of eighteen spiritual gifts most widely used by Bible scholars,[18] some with an alternative translation next to them. They are listed in no particular order. This is the list we will be working from. If your theological tradition adds or subtracts any from this list, please refer to your church's list as we move forward.[19]

Key Verse: "There are different kinds of working, but in all of them and in everyone it is the same God at work" (1 Cor. 12:6).

Passage of the Day: 1 Corinthians 12

Thoughts to Consider: The spiritual gifts point to two truths at the same time—unity and diversity. There are different gifts (diversity), but it is the same God (unity) who utilizes them for His purpose. In fact, as you read the passage, you no doubt noticed how strongly it directed us toward using this great variety of gifts toward a single, God-appointed purpose.

THE SPIRITUAL GIFTS

Prophecy (preaching)
Service (ministry)
Teaching
Exhortation (encouragement)
Giving (generosity)
Evangelism
Mercy
Wisdom
Knowledge
Faith
Healing
Miracles
Tongues
Interpretation of tongues
Discerning of spirits
Apostle
Shepherding (pastor)
Administration (leadership)

(From Romans 12:6–8; 1 Corinthians 12:8–10 & 28; Ephesians 4:11)

The spiritual gifts are given to us by God to do His work, not ours. As you consider the variety of spiritual gifts, think and pray about what gifts you have seen in operation when a church is functioning at it healthiest and best. Then take some time to pray that God will guide you and the church to reclaim that unity and diversity for God's glory as you move forward together.

DAY 32

Today's Big Idea: What are my spiritual gifts? Every follower of Jesus has at least one spiritual gift. That includes you. You may not know what those gifts are yet, you may not even fully believe you have any, but you do.

Key Verse: "We have different gifts, according to the grace given to each of us" (Rom. 12:6).

Passage of the Day: Romans 12:3–8

Thoughts to Consider: The opening verse of this passage is quite a bombshell, isn't it? Think of yourself using "sober judgment." This reminds me of one of our starting principles—the first task of a leader is to define reality. That's what the apostle Paul is telling us to do. Use sober judgment to understand who we are in Christ, including what spiritual gifts He has given us and how we might be called to use them.

There is so much to learn about the spiritual gifts in today's passage. Here are just a few points to consider: First, every Christian has at least one spiritual gift. Verse 3 tells us the gifts are "distributed to each of you," not just to some. Second, our gifts serve different functions, as we see in verse 4: "These members do not all have the same function." Third, a person's position in the church should be based on their gifts. Note that in verses 7–8, a person's giftedness (serving, teaching, encouraging) leads to their function (serve, teach, give encouragement).

The best way to serve the Lord with real purpose and joy is to find out what God has gifted you with, then do that!

This leads to a very important question that may have been nagging you: "What are my spiritual gifts and how can I discover them?" There are some helpful spiritual gifts assessments available (look for help at KarlVaters.com/100Days), but the best a written assessment can do is suggest a direction to consider or affirm what you already know. The most definitive way to discover your gifts is simple: start doing something! We discover our gifts by using them.

"But how do I use them it if I don't know what they are?" you may wonder. There's an old saying that goes, "God won't steer a parked car." If you want to be directed, you have to start moving first. Find a need and fill it. Hear a request for help and answer it. Listen to what respected leaders in your life have been telling you. Then experiment. Do what needs to be done, and as you do you'll start to discover what you do well, how you're of greatest blessing, and where you fit in the overall picture of the church. You may never know what to call your "gift mix" (a phrase Christians sometimes use to describe the collection of spiritual gifts a believer has), but it's more important to use them than to know what to call them.

For today, let's conclude our time by asking and answering the following questions as best we can:

What church activities have I been involved in with some degree of passion and effectiveness?

_____

_____

_____

_____

**Based on what I've already done in the
church, what spiritual gifts might I have?**

_____

_____

_____

_____

DAY 33

Today's Big Idea: What are the spiritual gifts of other church members? Thankfully, you're not the only person who's called to serve God through your local congregation. Every believer is called to do the same. Certainly, there will always be those who are more involved than others, but everyone should be doing something.

According to the Pareto principle, also known as the 80/20 rule, 80 percent of results will come from just 20 percent of the action.[20] In business, for instance, 80 percent of sales will come from 20 percent of customers, while 80 percent of new customers will be brought in by 20 percent of cold calls. In churches, this typically works itself out as 80 percent of the work of the church will be done by 20 percent of the congregation.

But typical results don't have to be inevitable results. God's principles are higher than the Pareto principle. And He has determined that everyone has a part to play in His body, the church.

Key Verse: "Be completely humble and gentle; be patient, bearing with one another in love" (Eph. 4:2).

Passage of the Day: Ephesians 4:1–8

Thoughts to Consider: Once again, unity is the focus of a passage about the spiritual gifts. When we consider the gifts, our focus is often about who's going to do what—and that's not a wrong way to look at them. In fact, we will spend a good deal of time on that, as the Scripture does. But God's primary concern with the operation of the gifts in the church is not about what we do, but how we treat each other.

Today's entire passage, which provides the lead-in context for a list of five leadership gifts,[21] is not about what the gifts will accomplish, but about how to watch out for each other, being patient and cooperative as we minister together. Those who are gifted to lead the church are commanded to "make every effort to keep the unity of the Spirit through the bond of peace" (Eph. 4:3).

Church Member	Their Possible Spiritual Gift(s)

As you consider how God wants to use spiritual gifts to accomplish His purposes in your congregation, take some time over the next week to consider the people you know in the church. What spiritual gifts have you seen in action? What do you believe they are or might be called to do? And, especially as this process moves forward, who seems especially gifted to work with this team to tackle the tasks that may be coming?

DAY 34

Today's Big Idea: What are some possible projects to consider? We've spent a Big Saturday coming to a clearer understanding of what the church does and all of this week considering the gifts God has deposited within the church body. This puts almost all the necessary ingredients on the table. Yes, *almost*.

On our next Big Saturday (Day 43) we will be choosing one project to tackle as a way of taking our first big step toward becoming a healthier church. By then, it will be very helpful for every member of the CLT to have a list of possible projects based on all the information we've gathered so far. These are what we'll start assembling, the last of the ingredients to go on the table.

Key Verse: "Suppose one of you wants to build a tower. Won't you first sit down and estimate the cost to see if you have enough money to complete it?" (Luke 14:28).

Passage of the Day: Luke 14:25–35

Thoughts to Consider: You doers on the team are probably thinking, "Yes! After all this navel-gazing, we're finally going to do something! Let's pick a project and get to work!" On the other hand, the more introspective folks on the team may be feeling a little apprehensive right now. "How can we pick a project when we haven't even decided on what issue we're going to tackle first?"

As we've seen in the Key Verse and Passage of the Day, it's important to strike a balance between the extremes of thinkers and doers. Sorry, go-getters, we won't be picking a project today, because your introspective friends are right. We don't have enough information to do that yet. But for my pondering friends, this is the time to start looking at actual forward motion. No, we don't have all the information we need (no project ever starts with *all* the information, after all), but we have enough to start brainstorming possible projects.

At this point, there's enough information to give most of you an idea of what possible issues the church might tackle as a team. So, as we did last Sunday with the church's current

Possible Issues	Possible Projects

activities and this week regarding spiritual gifts, let's make yet another list, this time of possible issues to tackle and possible projects to address them.

DAY 35 (SABBATH)

CHAPTER 9

Narrow
Your Options

Week 6

For the last seven days, we've been adding items to the top, wide end of the funnel. This week we'll narrow our options as we move toward the bottom of the funnel, concluding on Decision Day, this Saturday (Day 43). To do this, we need the right filter, a way of eliminating some options while keeping others.

One of the big temptations is to look around at what other congregations are doing and try to duplicate what's working well for them. They say imitation is the sincerest form of flattery, but it's one of the worst ways to build a great church. As we consider what to do, Jim Powell reminds us, "What worked for other congregations is irrelevant. If we don't address the culture of our churches, these cursory changes amount to little more than wasted money, wasted energy, and naïve optimism."[22] To move forward, we're not going to borrow ideas from somewhere else—although we can always learn from others—we're going to use what we already have.

Right now there's a lot on the table. In many ways, what we've done over the last five weeks may feel very much like part of the busy culture we looked at in chapter 3. It feels like busy work because it *is* busy.

It's like spring-cleaning. What was a fairly well-ordered home the day before seems like a madhouse on spring-cleaning day. Items that are usually in cupboards, in closets, and on shelves are out and scattered everywhere. A floor that's usually clear of junk is now littered with . . . is that trash? It looks like trash. Wait a minute, it *is* trash! There's *trash* all over the floor!

> SOMETIMES THINGS HAVE TO GET MESSIER BEFORE THEY GET CLEANER. YOU HAVE TO ASK HARD QUESTIONS TO GET TO SIMPLE ANSWERS.

Sometimes things have to get messier before they get cleaner. You have to ask hard questions to get to simple answers. That's where your church is right now—in the everything-is-on-the-floor-so-we-can-clean-inside-the-cupboards stage.

DAY 36 (SATURDAY)

Today's Big Idea: Keep, Give, or Toss? Now we start the process of sorting things out and putting them back in order. To do this in an actual housecleaning situation, organizational experts will ask the homeowner to divide their items into three stacks: *Keep It*, *Give It*, or *Toss It*.

Since everything in your church has now been hauled out

of the cupboards and onto the floor, metaphorically speaking, we're going to use the Keep-Give-Toss filter on them so we can arrive at Decision Day this coming Saturday with clearer minds and hearts. To do that, we'll spend the entire week walking through a single passage from the book of Acts in which the early church faced a problem and used the Keep-Give-Toss filter to simplify and solve it.

Key Verse: "It would not be right for us to neglect the ministry of the word of God in order to wait on tables. Brothers and sisters, choose seven men from among you who are known to be full of the Spirit and wisdom. We will turn this responsibility over to them" (Acts 6:2–3).

Passage of the Day: Acts 6:1–7

Thoughts to Consider: The first group of leaders in the early church were known as the Twelve. They were the disciples who had been closest to Jesus when He walked the earth (minus Judas, plus Matthias; Acts 1:23–26). Their primary assignment was to pray and teach the Word. It was a singular, narrowly defined task that guided everything they did.

Every church needs believers focused on tasks with narrow parameters. We must know what we're called to do, then narrow in on our assignment with a laser-tight focus. Unfortunately, the problems that inevitably come along can cause us to lose that focus. Then, after years of problems, challenges, and the constant drumbeat of everyday life, the mission can get lost in the mess.

This week's passage shows us one of the church's earliest challenges. It came in the form of a problem that threatened to divert the attention of the apostles from their primary assignment. They weren't tempted to do anything wrong or sinful. In fact, it was quite the opposite. The leaders were being called on to fill a need the church was supposed to keep as one of their primary emphases—the care of widows.

The Hellenistic widows (Jewish Christians who spoke Greek and were called from Jerusalem to reach Gentiles) complained that they weren't being treated as well as the Hebraic widows (Jewish Christians who spoke Hebrew and lived in and around Jerusalem) in the daily distribution of food. This problem needed to be solved, so the apostles proposed a solution. Pick seven people "who are known to be full of the Spirit and wisdom" and assign this important task to them. In this elegant solution, we see the principles of Keep-Give-Toss taking place. The apostles *Kept* true to their mandate to pray, study, and teach God's Word, *Tossed* the task from their personal to-do list, and *Gave* this important assignment to people better suited for the task.

Like the early apostles, your church does something well, or it can. But sometimes it takes solving a problem for that mission to come into clearer focus. That was true for the early church, just as it's true for your congregation. Let's pray today, as the early apostles did, that we will approach this important week wisely so we can make our decisions as well as the early church did.

DAY 37 (SUNDAY)

Today's Big Idea: KEEP your attention on Christ's mission.
In Weeks 1 and 2, we reaffirmed that Jesus is in charge of His

church. Therefore, anything and everything we do should start and end with God's will, not ours.

Key Verse: "The number of disciples was increasing" (Acts 6:1).

Passage of the Day: Acts 6:1–7

Thoughts to Consider: "The number of disciples was increasing." That doesn't sound like a problem, does it? Of course, it's not. But more people means more complexity, and more complexity means more problems—or at least new problems. That's what happened in the early church. The increased growth meant there were new challenges coming along.

That pattern has repeated itself throughout church history. We follow God, which brings blessings, then the blessings cause us to lose focus on the God who gave them.

In the first two weeks of this process, we reexamined Christ's mission for His church and our part in it. As we approach Decision Day, there will be other important tasks that will tend to draw our attention away from this. Take some time to consider what we need to do to assure that we keep our attention focused on Christ and His mission.

What do we need to do to KEEP Christ's mission as the focus of our attention?

_____

_____

_____

_____

_____

_____

_____

_____

_____

_____

_____

DAY 38

Today's Big Idea: KEEP meeting needs. The church has always been called to meet needs, especially the needs of the most vulnerable among us. First on that list are orphans and widows.

Key Verse: "The Hellenistic Jews among them complained against the Hebraic Jews because their widows were being overlooked in the daily distribution of food" (Acts 6:1).

Passage of the Day: Acts 6:1–7

Thoughts to Consider: Caring for widows and orphans is one of the central tenets of what James 1:27 calls "pure religion" (NLT). So when a problem developed in the distribution of food to widows, it couldn't be ignored.

Take some time to think and pray about the needs your church is called to meet, from inside the church to your local community, your region, and around the world. The meeting of needs can seem overwhelming, but every church is called to meet some of them. And if every congregation does their part, no one will be left out. As we see in Acts, the early church was so generous that, astonishingly, it was recorded that "God's grace was so powerfully at work in them all that there were no needy persons among them" (Acts 4:33–34). May it be so in our churches today.

What are the primary needs the church must KEEP meeting to stay true to our call?

_____

_____

_____

_____

_____

_____

_____

_____

_____

_____

_____

_____

DAY 39

Today's Big Idea: KEEP focused on your calling. In Weeks 3 and 4, we addressed the culture issue. What are the unwritten rules that govern what our church does—perhaps without us even being consciously aware of them? For this, maybe more than any other principle we look at this week, it's important to apply the Keep-Give-Toss filter.

Key Verse: "So the Twelve gathered all the disciples together and said, '*It would not be right for us to neglect the ministry of the word of God* in order to wait on tables'" (Acts 6:2, emphasis mine).

Passage of the Day: Acts 6:1–7

Thoughts to Consider: Studying and teaching God's Word was central to the mission and culture of the early church. And the apostles were the ones responsible to keep it in the center. They could not neglect it, even for something as important as feeding widows. As you consider the strengths of your church from Day 29, what stands out? What aspects of church life reinforce a positive culture? How can we keep them and strengthen them?

What does our church do *well* that we must KEEP doing?

_____

_____

_____

_____

_____

_____

_____

_____

_____

_____

DAY 40

Today's Big Idea: TOSS anything that diverts your attention. It's exciting to start a new ministry. It's brutally-hard to say goodbye to an old one. But we must. On spring-cleaning day, you may rediscover long-lost treasures as you dig deep into shelves, cupboards, and closets. It's tempting to want to keep all of it. But one of the central principles of spring-cleaning is to get rid of the clutter. First to go are items that can't be fixed or haven't been used in a long time.

Key Verse: "So the Twelve gathered all the disciples together and said, 'It would not be right for us to neglect the ministry of the word of God *in order to wait on tables*'" (Acts 6:2, emphasis mine).

Passage of the Day: Acts 6:1–7

Thoughts to Consider: Feeding widows was an essential ministry, but it wasn't what the apostles were called to do. So they made the hard but necessary decision to Toss it from their to-do list. (Don't worry, as we'll see tomorrow, the widows weren't forgotten.) It needed to be done, but not by them.

No church can do everything. We can't meet every need, function in every ministry, or make everyone happy. When we try to do it all we fail at what we should and could be doing well. One of the foundational building blocks of a church that is pursuing their calling with excellence is regularly making the hard decision to Toss what they don't do well.

What do we need to TOSS because it isn't being done well and can't be fixed—at least for now?

_____

_____

_____

_____

_____

_____

DAY 41

Today's Big Idea: GIVE the ministry away. As we saw in the verses we studied together way back on Day 1, Ephesians 4:11–12 tells us that the leaders of the church have a mandate from God, not to do all the ministry for the church but to equip God's people for works of service. We're supposed to give the ministry away.

Key Verse: "Brothers and sisters, choose seven men from among you who are known to be full of the Spirit and wisdom. We will turn this responsibility over to them and will give our attention to prayer and the ministry of the word" (Acts 6:3–4).

Passage of the Day: Acts 6:1–7

Thoughts to Consider: "We will turn this responsibility over to them." Those may be the hardest eight words in the world for some pastors to say, let alone to do. Give the ministry to others, along with responsibility and authority to make the decisions that need to be made.

But look who the apostles turned the ministry over to. It wasn't just anyone. The new recruits were full of the Spirit and wisdom, and they were "known" by the people for it. Their reputations were based on their character. Now they received the call.

Today, spend some time thinking and praying about who

we can equip to step up and take over ministry roles in the church, either for the first time or to a greater degree than they've attempted in the past. Consider their character, their spiritual life, and their ability to make wise decisions. Please note: giving these ministries away doesn't mean we stop doing them. That was dealt with yesterday in what we're tossing. Like the distribution of food to widows, the church will keep doing these ministries. It's just time for others to experience the joy of doing them.

What ministries can we GIVE to others, and who can we GIVE them to?

Ministries to GIVE away	People to GIVE them to
_____	_____
_____	_____
_____	_____
_____	_____
_____	_____
_____	_____
_____	_____
_____	_____

DAY 42 (SABBATH)

CHAPTER 10

Pick a Project

Week 7

DAY 43 (FOURTH BIG SATURDAY)
DECISION DAY

This is a big moment! It's the day we decide on a project to help our church become healthier.

Once again, begin with a time of prayer, followed by a short conversation about how the two weeks have gone since the previous Big Saturday. Have the daily devotionals been going well? Has everyone been observing their Sabbaths? If anyone has been having difficulty with them, offer encouragement, advice, and other assistance they might need, then pray for them to have greater success as we move forward.

Mission or Culture?

The first big decision of the day will be based on the principles we walked through in Week 3 (chapter 6) when we discovered

155

the importance of culture. It's time to decide if your project will fix a broken culture or move forward on mission.

As a reminder, a church's culture is the unwritten, often unrecognized set of rules that governs everything the congregation does. As we've already noted, knowing whether we need to fix the church's culture before moving forward on mission might be the most important question of the entire 100-Day process.

If your assessments in Week 3 showed that you have a culture problem with a Severity Score of 3 or higher, your decision has already been made for you. The culture issue must be dealt with first. The only real choice you have is whether to face this reality head on or keep ignoring it at your church's peril. A good mission simply will not grow in an unhealthy culture. Stop throwing good seed on bad soil. Fix the culture first.

Like the seed in the parable of the sower, the mission is always good, always available, and always up to Jesus, not us. What *is* up to us is how ready and willing our soil is to receive and give the mission a chance to thrive.

The quality of the seed is up to Jesus, not us, so it's always healthy and ready to grow. Create a healthy culture, and you'll have a healthy harvest.

The bulk of today's instructions will address that. We'll call it the Culture Track. After that, we'll offer guidance for the smaller group of churches whose culture is strong, to help them address specific issues of mission. That's the Mission Track.

After lunch, both tracks will follow the same format. But for the rest of the morning follow the track that fits your situation.

FOURTH BIG SATURDAY (DAY 43)

9 am: Intro and prayer
9:15–9:45 am: Mission or Culture?

THE CULTURE TRACK
9:45–10:15 am: Which Soil Are We?
10:15 am: Break
10:30–11:30 am: Changing the Soil
      Stubborn: Where does it hurt?
      Shallow: Where can we go deeper?
      Busy: Where do we simplify?

THE MISSION TRACK
9:45–11:30 am: More than Maintenance

11:30 am: Lunch
12:30–1 pm: What the Right Project
             Looks Like
1–1:45 pm: How to Pick Your Project
2–2:45 pm: Creating Project Teams (PTs)
2:45 pm: Closing comments and prayer
3 pm: Dismiss

Culture Track

Which soil are we? As we saw in Week 3 (chapter 6), Jesus addressed three specific culture issues in the parable of the sower: the Stubborn soil, the Shallow soil, and the Busy soil. In your assessments from that day, you arrived at a Soil Rating Score that told you which of the three soil issues you had and how severe that problem was. It will be helpful to have that chapter tabbed and ready to refer to as we walk through this session together.

Let's look at the soils again. If your church is dealing with more than one soil issue, read what you need for each of them.

Changing the soil. Nothing good will grow in bad soil. The bad dirt needs to be removed and replaced with healthy dirt. This is not about small tweaks to the programs, schedules, or style of the church. You won't turn an unhealthy culture into a healthy one by singing new songs, experimenting with different service times, or upgrading your facility.

> A CHANGE IN SOIL MEANS A CHANGE IN ATTITUDE—FROM STUBBORN TO ADAPTABLE, FROM SHALLOW TO DEEP, FROM BUSY TO SIMPLE.

A change in soil means a change in attitude—from Stubborn to Adaptable, from Shallow to Deep, from Busy to Simple. Let's get to work.

First soil: the Stubborn culture. Remember when we established that good soil becomes a hardened path after years of being trampled on by neglect and abuse? Instead of being treated as the valuable soil it is, it's been used by people with other agendas who were not looking out for the best interests of the soil. After years of such treatment, a church body becomes distrustful—especially if the hurt has been at the hands of leadership.

Change will take a softening of the soil and the heart. Of all the soils, this is the one that usually takes the longest to turn over. The sheer difficulty of effecting real change here is often a reason that the neglect of the soil has gone on for so long.

I have a pastor friend who has been at his church about five years. When he decided to become their pastor, the head of his denomination was shocked. "You want to go *there*!?" he asked. "Are you *sure*?" The reason for the stunned response was that this tiny church, tucked into the woods many miles outside a forgotten little town, had been through pastor after pastor for decades. They'd developed a reputation as a "pastor killer"—a church so hard, stubborn, and mean they'd chew up and spit out every pastor. My friend had many years of pastoral experience and a reputation that would have allowed him to pastor "better" churches. It made no sense for him to take on an impossible task in what was essentially a pastoral dumping ground. It's where the denomination would place pastors with little experience or who were recovering from a failure. But that repeated sending of underequipped leaders was, of course, one more big reason the church had grown hard and untrusting.

Thankfully, my friend saw what others refused to see. That little congregation wasn't a hostile church; it was a broken church. Today, five years later, the church is strong and healthy and has overcome the Stubborn reputation. They've responded to the care of a loving pastor and spouse who have been patient, kind, and gentle with them.

Most Stubborn churches aren't hostile, they're hurting. Even when they are hostile, it's usually in response to pain. The solution isn't to go in with guns blazing, only to cause more pain. We need to identify the hurt and heal it.

So if your church has a Stubborn culture, the first question to ask is the one that every doctor asks every patient when they show up with a complaint: Where does it hurt?

Stubborn soil: Where does it hurt? This is where the help of longtime church members will be a blessing to your CLT. In fact, if you're the pastor and this is your first read-through, take note of this point. If you think this might be your church's go-to issue, be sure to recruit some longtime church members who know the history of your church to be on the CLT.

For the rest of this morning's session, have a conversation. Start by asking the stalwart church members to share their stories and their hearts, to tell the group about the good old days. What was this church like when it was booming? What attracted you or your family to start attending? What has kept you here through the good times and bad?

Have them tell the group about the bad old days, too. When did things start turning for the worse? Did the troubles come from a single, traumatic event or from a slow process of bad decisions? Did it have to do with changes in the church or changes outside the church walls, like when the town's biggest employer closed down and people moved away?

Be prepared. Hurting people are seldom asked to speak, so when they start talking, they don't always speak well about their pain. They may complain about problems that seem old-fashioned, irrelevant, and outdated to you. That's okay. This isn't about finding solutions, it's about discovering pain points. When a patient tells a doctor, "It hurts when I jump up and down on my left leg," a good doctor doesn't say, "Then stop doing that!" They pay attention to what's hurting and why.

Identifying pain and its root causes requires disciplined, caring listening and learning from the entire team. Hear what's being said, not just on the surface, but a layer beneath the surface. If, for instance, they say something like, "It all started to go downhill when we stopped doing bus ministry." Your gut response might be, "Bus ministry? What in the world?" But this was a big deal in previous generations. When few people had access to adequate transportation, the church would pick up kids and families who had no way to get anywhere and bring them in for Sunday school and church. Bus ministry stopped when transportation was no longer a primary need for people. But a hurting person only knows that it worked then, but it's not working now.

So whether it's something old-school and outdated like a bus ministry, using hymnbooks instead of a projector, or wearing suits and ties instead of being casual, don't push back against the lamented issue. Listen to the pain beneath it. A complaint about stopping bus ministry is really a heartbreak over the loss of families. A longing for rejected hymnals may be about ending an old tradition without starting a new one. An expressed regret about casual clothes is likely about feeling disrespected. The pain isn't going to be fixed by going back to buses, hymnals, or suits and ties. We need to address the underlying issues of a passion for outreach, establishing new traditions, and treating the church's history with respect.

It's one thing to know where the pain is, it's another thing entirely to bring healing. The good news is, we have everything we need to do that. The Bible is filled with prescriptions for healing wounded hearts. Was the wound caused by sin? We need to repent—maybe as an entire church body. Neglect? Let them know Jesus has never rejected them, and back it up by pledging to renew your commitment to each other. Lack of resources? Rediscover God's provision.

Second soil: the Shallow culture. The second soil in Jesus' parable can be a very mysterious place to do ministry. On the surface, everything seems great. People get along. New people are welcomed. New ideas are embraced. Worship may be vibrant and alive. But year after year, nothing seems to get better. People come in readily, but they leave just as quickly. Remember that great idea from a few years back that everyone was excited about? Whatever happened to that? It never went anywhere. That pattern repeats itself over and over.

The Shallow church doesn't say "no" to anything. Good ideas aren't rejected, they slowly wither from lack of nourishment. The Shallow church culture is soft on the surface, but there's no depth, no maturity, nothing to sustain a deep root for the long term.

The Shallow church is an immature church. The answer is depth and maturity. But what, exactly, does your church need to go deeper in? In relationship? In worship? In discipleship? In outside-the-walls ministry? That's the next decision the Shallow church needs to make. Where do we need to go deeper?

Shallow soil: Where can we go deeper? When your CLT looks at all the information that's been put on your table over the last five weeks, literally and figuratively, what do you see? More importantly, what *don't* you see? What essential area of Christ's mission for His church is your congregation weakest in? If you look back to the exercise you did on your third Big Saturday (Day 29, in chapter 8), what types of ministries did you write in the "Do Less" column? What does it show the church to be shallow in?

One the Bible's great passages about the difference between a Shallow church and a Deep church is Hebrews 5:11–14. The author is obviously frustrated about the recipients' lack of maturity. They have been believers long enough that they "ought to be teachers," but instead they "need someone to teach you the elementary truths of God's word all over again." This is not because the people haven't been taught enough, but because they're not acting on what they know. Depth and maturity aren't about what you know; they come about because of what you *do* with what you know.

In the passage, the believers are told they need to be "teachers," "mature," and in "constant use" of what they know. Depth comes from doing, not from sitting and listening more. The author of Hebrews tells them they're still drinking milk because they can't handle solid food (*meat* in some translations). The difference between milk and solid food is simple. Milk has been through the cow.

A Shallow church may have a lot of Bible studies, but the members are relying on someone else to digest it for them and then they want more of the same. A mature church listens to good teaching, of course, but then decides to do something about it. They read the Bible for themselves. They share their faith with others. They get involved. They serve. Because that's what grown-ups do.

So take a look at where your church needs to go deeper.

We'll do that after lunch, based on the information we've collected in previous weeks. But remember to pay attention to what you *do*, not just what you learn. Move from being a teaching church to being an equipping church, from being passive to being active, from an inward focus to an outward focus, from "What's in it for us?" to "How can we be a blessing to others?"

Third soil: the Busy culture. When I arrived at my first pastorate—a small chapel in the California redwoods—I started my first week by getting my hands dirty with some much-overdue cleaning of the facility. First up, a nursery that had barely been used in years and an old, wooden crib with broken slats whose bare, sharp edges bent in toward the torn, dirty mattress. There was no question where this landed on the Keep-Give-Toss list.

As I was hauling the old crib out to the garbage, an elderly member drove by. "What are you doing there, pastor?" she asked, rolling down the window.

"I'm taking this broken crib to the garbage," I told her.

"Oh no," she responded. "That's not what we do here. We put broken furniture in that storage shed right there," she pointed. "It sits there for a few years until the rain coming through the leaky roof makes it all moldy and gross. Then we toss it out."

I looked up from hauling the crib to see a glint in her eye and a mischievous smile on her face. Unfortunately, not everyone has that senior church member's sense of humor or wisdom.

If your church has been around for twenty years or longer, your culture almost certainly has some Busy soil in it, some clutter that doesn't make any sense. But "That's the way we do things around here," right?

Life adds clutter. Sometimes the clutter is physical material, like old furniture and boxes of VBS materials that will never be used again. Often, it's activities we keep on the calendar even though they serve little or no purpose. Sometimes, it's systems, committees, and processes that would work better if they were streamlined—or axed.

If your church has a Busy culture, the answer is simple. Literally.

Busy soil: Where do we simplify? Remember that wall of butcher paper on Day 29, where you listed all the events, programs, and systems the church does? It filled up fast, didn't it? Start there. Pull out the photo you took of it or grab the original sheet of butcher paper and put it back on the wall.

That is your spring-cleaning floor. Today is the day to take all the items on that list and move them into one of three categories. You know what they are! Put another fresh sheet of butcher paper on the wall and write the three headings *Keep, Toss,* and *Give.*

But how do you decide which category each item belongs in? Here's a simple formula: If it it's an essential ministry item already being done by the people who must do it, put it under *Keep.* If it's an essential ministry item, but it can be done by someone other than the person(s) currently doing it—even if it will take some training first—put it under *Give.* Everything else (yes, *everything!*) goes in the *Toss* pile. After all, if you don't have someone who is already doing it well and there's no one who can do it well, it's time to stop trying.

On the first pass-through of assigning each item to the correct spring-cleaning column, the strategy is simple. Start with the items everyone agrees on. Take the items one at a time and ask everyone in the room to put up their hand for *Keep, Toss,* or *Give.* If an item gets a unanimous vote, it goes in that column. Have someone take note of the items that *almost* got full agreement, but tell the group, "We'll come back to that later."

After putting all the unanimous items in their Keep-Toss-Give columns, step back for a moment and ask the group this question: "What if we just made that happen?" Seriously. We often start the change process by tackling issues on which there's disagreement and controversy. But do we need to do that? Most of the time, we don't. Sure, there may be something that you *wish* was on the *Toss* list but that there's currently no agreement on. That's okay. You can't fix everything now. The point is to get things rolling, and the easiest way to get a stalled car moving is on a downslope. Start by going for the easy, early win. That will stimulate momentum, create enthusiasm, and encourage more change down the road.

If you didn't find enough unanimous agreement in that first go-around to move ahead with, take another pass-through with the items that got a near-unanimous vote. Start by asking, "How severe is the disagreement on this?" If it's strong, skip that item and move to the next. If the disagreement is mild, have a conversation about what can be done to come to an agreement. It may be a misunderstanding about the item, the terminology, or something else that can be resolved quickly. If so, come to an agreement and add it to the correct column.

At this point, you may be wondering, "Does every decision

need to be unanimous?" In general, no. Requiring a unanimous decision can cripple forward progress. But if you can get it, why not start there? These changes will be hard enough, anyway. If we can make it easier by making changes everyone agrees on, you'll significantly increase your chance of success.

In fact, let's take one last look at the passage we've spent our entire week looking at together. After the decision was made to assign the seven to oversee the distribution of food to widows, it is noted that "This proposal pleased the whole group" (Acts 6:5). Did that happen because they took a poll with a unanimous result? Not likely. But in this situation, which sets so many great examples for how we should behave as a church going forward, even though a small group of leaders made the decision, it mattered what the rest of the group thought of that decision. That group very likely included those who would be affected by the decision, and they were pleased.

Now let's get back to the business at hand. Once more, after going through the list and moving more items into the Keep-Toss-Give columns, step back and look at the wall again. By now, it's likely that there are enough items on the list to put a project together and take some positive steps forward.

If you can't get enough items on the wall to create a doable project from the first two passes, then you probably have a Stubbornness culture issue to deal with in addition to the Busy soil. If so, the Stubbornness issue needs to be dealt with first, so refer back to that.

Mission Track

Now we move to the track for the small percentage of churches that have a healthy culture and are ready to receive the seed and move forward on mission. (I say this is a small percentage of churches not because I think most churches in the world are not missional or healthy, but because if you're reading a book entitled *100 Days to a Healthier Church* it's probably not because things are going great. And the vast majority of the problems in unhealthy churches are culture issues.)

Who are we? On the Culture Track, we asked, "What kind of soil are we?" But if your culture is healthy enough that you're ready to work on mission, we know what kind of soil you are. You're the fourth soil, the soft, deep, weed-free, healthy soil. Your church isn't perfect. No church is. But if your culture is strong, the soil is healthy enough that the right mission planted at the right time and nurtured in the right way has a wonderful chance of being very successful for Christ and His kingdom.

More than maintenance. So what are the characteristics of a church with a healthy culture? Let's look at four of them.

First, the people in a healthy culture know the church doesn't exist for its own self but for God's glory. No farmer works hard to keep a field healthy just so they can say, "Look! A healthy field!" They do it to produce a harvest. But we do that in the church sometimes. We work on systems, structures, and programs, then step back and admire what we've done, as if enjoying the admiring was the point. It's not. A church that stays focused on itself is a mockery to God and His mission. We're called to have more than a well-maintained facility, a strong budget, and a well-organized Sunday morning service. A healthy church exists to glorify God and to produce something of value for Christ and His kingdom.

These reasons to exist lead us right to the second characteristic of a healthy culture: healthy soil produces a harvest.
There's a popular but problematic notion that the only way to
help a church become healthier is to find what's broken and fix
it. Certainly, there are benefits to doing that, especially when
there are problems deep in the culture. Those problems should
always be fixed. But if you have a healthy culture, staying in the
mode of fixing problems is like the farmer with a well-plowed
but empty field. Fixing problems, by definition, keeps a church
in maintenance mode. We've got to do more than that. We have
to plant seed and nurture a harvest.

To move from maintenance into healthfulness we need to
lean into the third characteristic of a healthy culture—being
a blessing to others. Like a healthy field, the harvest from a
healthy church doesn't stay where it was planted; it blesses
others. We're not just supposed to do ministry *in* the church,
we're called to ministry *from* the church.

This leads to the fourth characteristic of a healthy culture.
In addition to producing a harvest, a healthy culture produces
seeds for next year's harvest. As the old saying goes, "Anyone
can count how many apples are on a tree, but only God knows
how many trees are in an apple." The healthiest churches don't
just produce this season's harvest, they develop habits and practices that will perpetuate a harvest year after year. For instance,
if your ministry departments are chronically short of volun-
teers or leaders, or if your church is constantly concerned about
hiring people to handle the tasks of ministry instead of raising
up your own leaders, you're not planting leadership seeds for

the future. Healthy churches equip disciples to lead the church from one season to the next.

How well is your church pursuing those four characteristics? For your next exercise, put another sheet of butcher paper on the wall. Divide it into four columns, one for each of the following questions based on the four characteristics of a healthy church culture:

1. Are we existing for ourselves, or for the glory of God?
2. Are we producing a harvest? If so, what is that harvest?
3. Are we doing ministry *from* the church or is it concentrated *in* the church?
4. Do we have habits and practices that create seeds for the future?

Pose these questions to the CLT and write the group's answers down. After that, ask, "What area(s) do we need the most improvement on? And what are some ideas for making those improvements?"

What the Right Project Looks Like

This is it! The moment all the doers on the team have been waiting for. It's time to pick a project and turn all this talk, prayer, study, and conversation into real-life hard work. Let's review seven parameters for a great church project.

First, any project must meet God's approval. We spent our first two weeks obsessing over this point. It's Jesus' church, so every goal, every idea, and every project must start and end with His plans, not ours. If a project doesn't fit what Jesus wants for His church, we can't do it. No matter how cool the project is or how comfortable it makes us.

Second, the best projects rely on God's participation. Once we get into project mode it's easy just to rely on the plan, as if our structures and systems are enough to make our church healthy, strong, and vibrant again. But as important as it is to have a plan, it's just as important not to overplan. Leave God room to do something unexpected.

Andy Stanley may be one of the most well-known planners in church leadership, but even he says, "It is dangerous to become too preoccupied with trying to figure out how to bring about your vision. Plan the best you can. But remember, a divine vision necessitates divine intervention."[23]

Third, a project is not necessarily an event. To give you a sense of what a non-event-based project looks like, here are three projects our church has done using the principles in this book, each of which highlights a different type of change.

A change in attitude. For years, I led our church in pursuing numerical growth based on what we learned from church growth principles. But we saw almost none of the promised results. This led to a long, difficult season for me and the church in which we questioned everything, including our reason for existing and my call to ministry.[24] To come out of that difficult season, we needed a change in attitude. So that was our project: to discover and use the principles we needed to become a healthy small church, not just a bigger church.

A change in emphasis. There was a season in which we

realized the church was doing well, but we weren't being challenged to stretch ourselves. We needed to pull ourselves out of that place of comfort by reworking how we did ministry in three key areas: worship, fellowship, and leadership. The project that got us there was to implement a change in emphasis. We experimented with various modes of worship, we created new opportunities for fellowship, and we adapted to new methods for training our leaders. It was an exciting and frustrating time of experimentation, but the long-term results produced greater effectiveness in all three areas.

A change in direction. Our most recent project was our biggest one yet, a pastoral transition. After twenty-five years as the lead pastor of Cornerstone, I moved aside to become the teaching pastor so that Gary Garcia, my youth pastor for that entire twenty-five-year period, could step up as our new lead pastor. This project was not an event or a program; it was a change in direction. For twenty-five years, Cornerstone was led by my leadership gifts with Gary's in a support position. But after twenty-five years, we as a church (starting with the two of us leaders) realized it was time for us to go in a direction more suited to having Gary lead, with me supporting him.

Fourth, the project must be visible. For a project to be successful, you have to get people working on it. And to work together, there must be something visible to work toward. For instance, "Be better worshipers" is a great goal, but how will you know if you've done it? That idea has to be filtered through a visible project like a change in musical style, adding a new service, or changing the order of your current service.

Fifth, the project should be memorable. When you're in

the middle of a long project, it can be easy to lose your way, and even forget what you're supposed to be doing. So the project needs a name everyone can recall quickly and that inspires forward motion. I'm usually not a big fan of alliterations or rhymes, especially in sermons. But a simple alliteration or rhyme can be an important way to make a project memorable.

Sixth, the success of the project must be definable. When doing a project with a team, clear boundaries are your friend. Every team within the project needs to know what they are and are not supposed to do. You need clear time-stamped goals along the way. Dates must be put on the calendar. Facility usage must be assigned. Team members must be on a roster. And everyone needs to know who has the final say in various aspects of the project departments.

Seventh, the project must be flexible and adaptable. Any army that goes into battle without a plan will lose. But the moment the battle starts, the plan will change. Every general knows that. So if the plan is going to change when the battle begins, why have a plan at all? Because a battle without a plan to adapt from is a battle you will lose. The initial plan is based on a goal that isn't going to change, but it must have moving parts that can be adapted to new information and events.

How to Pick Your Project

Now that we know what a project should and shouldn't be, how exactly do we go about choosing one right here, right now? Here's what I've learned about working on a large, important issue: coming up with five ideas is easier than coming up with one!

First, don't look for one great idea, look for a few pretty good ideas. If you ask somebody to name their favorite movie or the best meal they ever had, they tend to freeze up. It's hard to identify one clear favorite. But if you ask for five favorite foods or five favorite movies, they'll start rattling off a list—and they may not stop at five.

Asking people to pick one project is intimidating. So have your team take a few private moments to independently list five possible projects they think might be doable, given all the information you've currently assembled. Encourage them not to worry yet about applying the seven project requirements.

After they've had time to write down some ideas, open the floor for discussion, writing everything on our friendly neighborhood butcher paper. As usual, there are no bad ideas. Just get them out in front of everyone.

Second, apply the seven principles as a sort of filter to each potential idea. Take up the ideas on the wall one at a time. Start crossing off ideas that don't meet several major criteria. If some are close to meeting all the criteria, ask if there's a way to get those ideas all the way there.

Third, pick one—just one. Sometimes that single project will come from a blending of two or more ideas, but they have to be boiled down into a single project. If you get stuck on more than one good project possibility, apply one more filter to them: "Which of these ideas is most likely to be a success?" It's better to start with something you know can succeed at than to start with something bigger and more important that may not work.

Finally, don't stress out because your project is less than

perfect. They're all less than perfect! One of my favorite Bible verses about planning is found in Acts 15. During what became known as the Jerusalem Council, the disciples went back and forth about which laws Gentile converts would be required to keep. When they finally came up with what many theologians believe to be an imperfect compromise solution, they presented it to the group with these words: "It seemed good to the Holy Spirit and to us" (Acts 15:28).

That feels like almost every church planning meeting I've been in. We almost never come up with an idea that feels like a true home run. Usually, it's *seems* good. It's an idea that we can get behind. It *seems* like the Lord may be in it. Are we sure? Not always. But we feel close enough that we're ready to give it a shot. Sometimes "close enough" has to be enough.

Creating Project Teams

The final task for this momentous day is to make the project doable by dividing it into tasks, choosing leaders for each task, deciding on team members for each task, considering costs and needed resources, and coordinating dates.

Have you run out of butcher paper yet? I hope not. Because you'll need another sheet for this. Write the project name on the top, then a series of columns where you'll put the names of tasks, plus space for a master timeline and smaller, task-specific timelines. Eventually, these should make their way to a master calendar that everyone can access, either electronically or physically, but the butcher paper will allow space for working things out.

Divide the project into tasks. Accomplishing your chosen project requires planning. The central aspect of planning is dividing one big task into a group of small tasks. There are two ways those tasks can be divided—chronologically and operationally. Every big project requires a combination of the two.

Chronological tasks are those that must be done by a certain time. The team must be assembled by this date, the resources purchased by this date, the launch will be scheduled on this date, and so on. Operational tasks run side by side on the calendar, with different teams completing different tasks, but all coming together at certain points along the way. For instance, most projects will have a performance (on stage) team, a setup and teardown team, advertising, recruiting, fundraising, and so on. In smaller churches, or on smaller sections of the project, some tasks will be done by individuals, not teams. And some people will serve on multiple tasks and teams.

One team that will need to be created, even though they won't get into full gear until later, is the Celebration Team. These are the people who will be in charge of planning, promoting, and running the Celebration Day on Day 100, after the project has been completed.

On the butcher paper, give each task a column under the project title.

Choose a leader for each task. Once the main tasks have been decided on, the CLT needs to determine who will be in charge of the entire project, and which members will oversee the various tasks. These decisions should be based on skill, willingness, and availability, not titles or positions. So divide the project into tasks first so you'll know who you need based on the specific tasks.

Write each leader's name in the column under their assigned task.

Decide on team members for each task. Most tasks will need more than just an assigned leader but also a team behind that leader. In most churches, especially smaller ones, the team members will be obvious. But discuss the possibilities, and make sure various task leaders aren't planning to tap the same people for their teams. While a person could serve on more than one team, schedules will have to be coordinated and responsibilities accepted.

Add those names under the leader's name in their task column.

Start thinking about costs and needed resources. Some tasks will take hours, but no money. Some will take almost no time, but cost money. Other tasks will need furniture, equipment, and other materials. Start writing up these details in their respective task columns so shared resources can be coordinated, facility usage can be balanced, and a budget can be designed. If the project will require a large expense that will necessitate raising money or approving a budget, you might need to implement the Pause Point coming after Day 49 to allow time for fundraising or budget adjustments. (Pastor, if your church has extremely limited funds or has a complicated policy for budget approvals, you may want to get your finance team in place so they can make needed decisions quickly without slowing down the process.)

DAY 44 (SUNDAY)

Today's Big Idea: Nehemiah's call to rebuild the temple.
There may be no better example of how to pull a team of people together to restore a place of ministry and worship than the story of Nehemiah rebuilding the walls of Jerusalem. So we will spend this entire week looking at the details of this important task.

Key Verse: "If it pleases the king and if your servant has found favor in his sight, let him send me to the city in Judah where my ancestors are buried so that I can rebuild it" (Neh. 2:5).

Passage of the Day: Nehemiah 2:1–9

Thoughts to Consider: Nehemiah was a Jew, but he was born a captive in the foreign land of Persia (modern-day Iraq). When he heard the news that Jerusalem, the home city of his ancestors, was in ruins, he was saddened. Like Nehemiah, many people in the church will be inspired into action in a similar way. They may not even remember the days when the church was thriving, but it's their home, so when they feel sad that it's not all it could be, that godly sorrow should spur them to action.

Just like the king gave Nehemiah the authority he needed to do the task, so God has done that for us. As you take some time to share your burden for your church, remember to honor its past, sorrow over its current needs, and express hope for its future. Nehemiah felt and expressed all of those, and it set him on the path for a successful enterprise.

There are Nehemiahs in your church. Ask God for the eyes to see who they are and call them into action. If a pagan king can be used by God to recognize the godly sorrow in Nehemiah, he can use you to see the same sorrow and the same call in others.

(Note for the pastor: Depending on the nature of your project and other factors in your church, today is likely the day you'll announce the project to the church body and start recruiting Project Team members. This will happen either through voluntary sign-ups, specific requests, or a combination of the two.)

DAY 45

Today's Big Idea: Nehemiah inspects the wall. Starting today, your Project Team leaders will be making phone calls and sending emails to people who signed up to help, and those they plan to recruit. One of the best recruiting tools is the fact that you have a project and the start of a plan based on weeks of hard work.

Key Verse: "The God of heaven will give us success. We his servants will start rebuilding" (Neh. 2:20).

Passage of the Day: Nehemiah 2:10–20

Thoughts to Consider: Instead of jumping right in and acting like he knew it all, Nehemiah quietly and deliberately took the necessary time to inspect the condition of the wall, so he would know the scope and severity of the task that was ahead of him. That's exactly what the CLT has been doing over the past six weeks.

At the end of the inspection, Nehemiah had all the information he needed to start rebuilding, and the confidence that the Lord would give them success in it. That's where your church is right now. The work hasn't begun yet, but you're far more ready to face it wisely than you were six weeks ago. Take some time to reflect back on what you've learned, how far you and the rest of the CLT have already come. Even though you may have already faced some opposition and, like Nehemiah, you will likely face some more, the good news far outweighs the bad. Know that God will give you success as you start rebuilding.

DAY 46

Today's Big Idea: Nehemiah assigns positions on the wall. Nehemiah was called to rebuild the wall, but he knew he couldn't do it himself. Every great effort needs a team. Yours may not be the team you expect. They may not have the skills you think you need. But when Jesus said He'd build His church, He knew who He would need. And He knows what and who you'll need, too.

Key Verse: "Rephaiah son of Hur, ruler of a half-district of Jerusalem, repaired the next section. Adjoining this, Jedaiah son of Harumaph made repairs opposite his house" (Neh. 3:9–10).

Passage of the Day: Nehemiah 3

Thoughts to Consider: The detailed list of repairs to the wall and the people who did them is a breathtaking lesson in cooperation, sacrifice, and skill. Some repaired the section of the wall closest to their house, while others came from faraway tribes and nations. Those working on the wall were rich and poor, leaders and servants, men and women, priests and laity, builders and merchants.

When considering who should serve on the upcoming Project Teams, don't leave anyone out. In situations like this, it's often the least likely people who do the greatest work.

DAY 47

Today's Big Idea: Nehemiah faces opposition. No great work goes on without opposition. Sometimes it's external, sometimes it's internal. But it always comes. But remember that the presence of opposition does not mean the absence of God. **Key Verse:** "They were all trying to frighten us, thinking, 'Their hands will get too weak for the work, and it will not be completed.' But I prayed, 'Now strengthen my hands'" (Neh. 6:9). **Passage of the Day:** Nehemiah 4 and 6

Thoughts to Consider: Nehemiah's enemies didn't attack him or the workers head on. They employed scare tactics, then delay tactics. But Nehemiah wouldn't be diverted from the task God had called him to. Instead of praying that the burden be lifted, Nehemiah prayed that his hands would be strengthened. As this project moves forward, there will be challenges, even outright attacks. The goal of those attacks will be to stop your work from reaching its goal. But remember this—if God called you, He will strengthen you.

DAY 48

Today's Big Idea: Nehemiah demonstrates character and maintains his priorities. When you engage in a big project, it can be easy to lose sight of the big picture. Needs that are immediate and urgent seem more important than a mission that's long-term and hard to see. In today's passage, Nehemiah faced such a temptation and showed us how to face it with our priorities and character intact.

Key Verse: "I never demanded the food allotted to the governor, because the demands were heavy on these people" (Neh. 5:18).

Passage of the Day: Nehemiah 5

Thoughts to Consider: This passage shows us one of the reasons God chose Nehemiah for this great task. It wasn't just because Nehemiah had great leadership skills—although he did—but because he had such strong character. While the people were building the wall and preparing to defend themselves from outside attackers, there was a great evil being perpetrated from within. Because many of the workers were giving up their regular employment to work on the wall, they were mortgaging their land to borrow money to pay their daily bills. A group of their fellow countrymen were taking advantage of this by charging high interest rates, then foreclosing on them, even enslaving their children when they couldn't pay on time.

When Nehemiah heard about this, he was understandably incensed. He demanded that their families, land, and property be returned, and that the moneylenders stop charging interest on their loans. They agreed, and the work went forward. Then, Nehemiah made sure to let everyone know that he never behaved that way. In fact, he even gave up the extravagant food that was rightfully his so those in greater need could have it instead.

There will be times during this process when it will be tempting to ignore the needs of the people in order to complete the project. But we church leaders must always remember this: Our church people aren't the raw material we use to complete the project. The people are the point of the project—people loving Jesus, loving each other, and sharing the good news. No wall, no church building, and no project is more important than that.

DAY 49 (SABBATH)

Pause Point

Since this is the week you'll be announcing the project to the church, making calls, and getting people signed up to help out, it may be a good time to hit Pause on the 100-Day process. After all, if you need a lot of people on your Project Teams, it will take them time to coordinate their schedules for the busy season that's coming.

If this is your first read-through of this book, take note of this day. When you actually start walking through this process with your team, it will be helpful to have this possible Pause Point in mind so you can properly prepare for it. As a leader, you'll probably be thinking of who might be on your project teams long before you get to this day. Call them in advance to find out if they can clear their schedule so you know they'll be ready when called on.

There are some leaders in your church who will be suited to walk through the entire 100 Days with you, while others, who may also be capable and mature leaders, will serve the church best by coming in for the final fifty-day push. In some cases, you may want someone on the CLT for the entire 100 Days, but their schedule only allows for them to be in for the last fifty. In still other cases (although this should be rare) there might be someone who will be with you for the first fifty days, but not the last fifty. In other words, arranging these teams may require time, so your first read-through of this book gives you this heads-up notice that this point is potentially a place to take more time. Whatever happens, don't let this day sneak up on you.

Pause Points should be temporary and limited—and not allowed to become delays. Make sure Day 51 comes back onto the calendar within a week or two. Don't make the mistake of saying, "We'll put this on hold until we figure a few things out." This allows too great an opportunity for the 100 Days never to be completed and to end up yet another false start. Instead, say, "Let's recruit our Project Teams and start back up with Day 50 on this specific date on the calendar."

Deadlines have a way of inspiring initiative, maintaining momentum, and encouraging forward motion. The deadline also communicates to the team that the Pause is intentional and not a lingering delay.

A Big Shift

The first fifty of the 100-Days project has been laid out like a blueprint, with a lot of detailed and precise directions. But the next fifty days are more about your church's specific, individual project, so the guidelines will be limited and more like a suggestion box than like a detailed blueprint.

To switch metaphors, this is when I'll be taking my hand off the back of your bicycle to let you and your CLT balance yourself as you move forward. After all the work you and your CLT have done, your bicycle has enough momentum to stay upright as you create a project that's unique and specific to your congregation. So as the training wheels come off, keep pedaling! I'll be less involved, but there will still be signposts along the way.

STEP 3

Train the Team

"And each one of you is a part of it."

1 Corinthians 12:27

CHAPTER 11

Expand Your Leadership Circle

Week 8

U ntil now, the Core Leadership Team has been praying, pondering, and planning. You've thought long and hard about what Christ wants for His church, where your church is, where you need to go, and what some first steps will be to help you get there.

To revisit our painting metaphor from earlier, the colors have been decided, the walls have been sanded, the edges have been taped, and the tarp has been spread. Now it's time for the painters to start applying the paint. The hands-on work begins.

You'll spend the next few weeks working with your project team and training them to be ready when the project is finally launched.

DAY 50
(FIRST ALL-TEAM BIG SATURDAY)

As you start today with prayer, help the new folks in the room get familiar with what's been happening so far. Tell them about the daily Bible devotional and how you've been holding each other accountable to observe a one-in-seven Sabbath. They'll be sharing these experiences with you over the remaining fifty days.

As you check in with the CLT members about how they've been doing with their daily devotionals and Sabbath-keeping, show the new team members that this accountability is about encouragement and support, not criticism and guilt.

What Kind of Church Are We?

After that opening time of prayer and encouragement, let them know the broad outline of the day. The morning will be spent taking an overview of what's happened in this process so far, bringing everyone up to speed. There's a lot of ground to cover, so they'll need time to catch up, ask questions, and process information.

Begin at Day 1. Take half an hour or so to explain to the group why this process was started, how the CLT came together, and—most importantly—what you've learned about what Jesus says about His church. Tell them how you spent an entire day exploring Scripture together to rediscover what the Bible says about the church. This would be a great time to have CLT members recall what they learned that day.

FIRST SATURDAY ALL-TEAM MEETING (DAY 50)

9 am: Intro and prayer
9:15–10:30 am: What Kind of Church Are We?
    What Jesus' church is 9:15–9:40 am
    What our church is 9:40–10:05 am
    What our church needs 10:05–10:30 am

10:30 am: Break
10:45–11:30 am: Why Are You Here?
    How we decided the project 10:30–11 am
    How the teams are set up 11–11:30 am

11:30 am: Lunch
12:30–1:30 pm: Individual Team Meetings
    Our assignment 12:30–1 pm
    Your role: 1–1:30 pm

1:30 pm: Break
1:45–2:45 pm: What's Next?
    Team reports: 1:45–2:15 pm
    Final adjustments: 2:15–2:45 pm
2:45 pm: Closing comments and prayer
3 pm: Dismiss

After that, take another half hour to walk with them through Weeks 1 and 2. Show how you asked hard questions about your congregation—how you explored its history, its present-day condition, and your hopes for its future. Spread out the butcher papers you worked on together so the newcomers can see the important principles of the different church cultures, the Life Cycle of a church, and how you discovered where your church landed on them. The visuals provided by the butcher paper, all marked up with ideas, thoughts, changes, and corrections, is a great way for them to understand that what they're being introduced to is not a whim or the ideas of some guy (me) in some book they've never heard of (this one), but that your team has been investing hard work and careful, prayerful attention to your church's future. Again, this is a wonderful time for the members of the CLT to share their thoughts about what they've learned, challenges they've overcome, and how some of their original doubts and concerns have been answered.

Then take another thirty minutes or so to show the new team members how all this information came together to help the CLT understand what your church needs to do to move forward in health and effectiveness.

After this hour-and-a-half flyover of the first four weeks, everyone will need a break.

Why Are You Here?

After the break, reassemble everyone to answer the all-important question, "Why are we here today?" Take the next hour before lunch to describe the process you walked through as a CLT in Weeks 5 through 7 in order to decide on the project (again, show them the butcher paper), how you decided on tasks, teams, leadership—in other words, how you came to ask them to serve (or how you opened it up for them to volunteer to serve).

During lunch, have the CLT members make themselves

available to the newcomers to answer questions. The church's best asset today may not be what's said by the pastor during the sessions, but what they hear and feel from regular church members during the breaks and lunch, or after the day is over.

INDIVIDUAL TEAM MEETINGS

Following lunch, individual teams can meet with their team leaders. This will be their first chance to see who they'll be working with, to hear from their team leader, and to talk together about their particular assignment. If people are on more than one team, have them meet with the team that requires the most explanation or the one in which they'll be taking a greater leadership role.

After giving team members an overview of expectations, break down the roles of each individual, including conversation and coordination with other team members. Start looking at timelines, what resources will be needed, any problems they foresee, and what their first steps will be.

WHAT'S NEXT?

Finally, after another short break, gather everyone so each team can give a report about their conversation, what they'll be needing, problems the team discovered, and how all the teams will coordinate together.

Before you dismiss, remind the new team members how central the devotionals and Sabbath days have been to this process, and encourage them to participate by following them for the next 50 Days. Some of these new team members won't have copies of this book, but the devotionals are available online for free (at KarlVaters.com/100Days).

DAY 51 (SUNDAY)

The process of *100 Days to a Healthier Church* is now past the halfway point. For the first fifty days, the CLT shared a lot of reading, talking, planning, and prayer. Now you'll do far less reading, talking, and planning, but a lot more hands-on work. The prayer continues! From now on, your reading and daily devotions will provide a timeline and inspirational nudges to keep first things first, but all of that is subject to adjustment, depending on your specific project.

Today's Big Idea: One body with many parts. If you're new to this team and this is your first devotional day with us, welcome! You'll find each day to be short, biblical, practical, and applicable to the task at hand—helping the church you serve become healthier in the next 50 Days.

Key Verse: "Just as a body, though one, has many parts, but all its many parts form one body, so it is with Christ" (1 Cor. 12:12).

Passage of the Day: 1 Corinthians 12:12–31

Thoughts to Consider: Our Passage of the Day is really the Passage of the Week. Every day, we'll use this passage to learn how we, the church, can work together under the lordship of Christ.

Today's Key Verse tells us that the church of Jesus exists in both unity and harmony. Like your physical body has hands, legs, feet, blood cells, nerves, and a heart, the body called the church has different parts, too. While each body part does a different task, they all do something important, united under the head—that is Christ. We're not all the same. We're not supposed to be. But we all serve the body.

Take some time to reflect on and pray about your part in the body and to thank the Lord that no one else serves quite the way you do.

DAY 52

On Day 17, the members of the Church Leadership Team (those who have been in this process since Day 1) were asked to remember and write down how they felt and what they thought about the church at the start of this process. Today, new members of the Project Teams are encouraged to do the same.

If you're a member of the CLT, let your team members know you're available to them as they work through this process like you did.

Today's Big Idea: Don't despise your role. Have you ever felt unimportant because you don't have the same role as someone else in the church, like a teacher, a worship leader, or the pastor? Today is the day to give those feelings to Jesus.
Key Verse: "Now if the foot should say, 'Because I am not a hand, I do not belong to the body,' it would not for that reason stop being part of the body" (1 Cor. 12:15).
Passage of the Day: 1 Corinthians 12:12–31
Thoughts to Consider: It's an interesting picture the apostle

Paul draws here, isn't it? Imagine one of your feet thinking it's not of any value because it's not a hand. The sad reality is, we do that in the church. But in Christ's church no gift is more important than any other, which means the reverse is also true—no gift is *less* important than any other.

Jesus made you as you are. There's no unimportant part of the body. There may be some parts that are less visible, but they all matter to Jesus—and they all matter in His church. You matter.

DAY 53

Today's Big Idea: Don't despise the roles of others. As we saw yesterday, we can easily despise the role we play in the church. And if we don't deal with those feelings in a healthy, biblical way we often turn those toxic feelings outward to others.

Key Verse: "The eye cannot say to the hand, 'I don't need you!' And the head cannot say to the feet, 'I don't need you!' On the contrary, those parts of the body that seem to be weaker are indispensable" (1 Cor. 12:21–22).

Passage of the Day: 1 Corinthians 12:12–31

Thoughts to Consider: You are "indispensable." I didn't say that, the Bible does. So is every other part of the body of Christ, known as the church. In fact, like the human body, the parts that seem weakest and most vulnerable are often the most important for the functioning of a healthy body.

Have you ever looked at someone else's role in the church and devalued them? "They're too young to matter." "They're too old to be relevant." "They have different theological positions from mine so they must not be a mature Christian—maybe they're not a Christian at all!" The truth is, only God knows the heart. It's not our job to judge others, it's our command to love them. You're indispensable. They're indispensable. Loving one another is indispensable.

DAY 54

Today's Big Idea: Value the roles of others. When was the last time you went out of your way to thank someone in the church who does something behind the scenes?

Key Verse: "God has put the body together, giving greater honor to the parts that lacked it, so that there should be no division in the body, but that its parts should have equal concern for each other" (1 Cor. 12:24–25).

Passage of the Day: 1 Corinthians 12:12–31

Thoughts to Consider: God despises division in the church. One of the biggest causes of division is when we don't value the role everyone plays in the body. This is especially true of people who serve in areas that aren't as visible as others. The pastor and worship leader get thanked a lot (and criticized, too). But what about the person running the sound board? The only time we even think about them is when something goes wrong. Before leaving this devotional, think about someone in your church who works behind the scenes and take a moment to thank them. Right now. Send them a text, an email, or give them a phone call.

Did you do it? Great! You may now get on with the rest of your day.

DAY 55

Today's Big Idea: Value your role. You matter. Yes, you.
Key Verse: "Now you are the body of Christ, and each one of you is a part of it" (1 Cor. 12:27).
Passage of the Day: 1 Corinthians 12:12–31
Thoughts to Consider: The word *you* appears twice in today's Key Verse. The first one is a plural, like when my Southern friends say "y'all" or "all y'all." It refers to the church as a gathered group. The second "you" is singular—as in just you, by yourself. Both *yous* matter. When we gather on Sunday to worship, fellowship, and minister together, we are the body of Christ. When you're all alone on Monday, or perhaps in an environment that's neutral, even hostile to the gospel, you are just as much a part of the body. We are always connected to each other through Christ's body. Never forget that, and be grateful.

DAY 56 (SABBATH)

A quick note for those who are new to these daily devotionals. Today's your day off. For one day every week, we take a Sabbath, like God commanded in the Ten Commandments. It's your day to rest, slow down, and do something else. Certainly, you should still spend time in God's Word and prayer, but for this day, we give everyone a break from thinking and working on the *100 Days to a Healthier Church* process.

We'll see you tomorrow!

CHAPTER 12

Adjust the Plan

Week 9

When you think of the word *genius,* what's one of the first names that comes to mind? Albert Einstein is on the top of that list, right? Of course. Even when we're being sarcastic about a friend's mistake, we say, "Nice work, Einstein!" But, smart as he was, even that great genius made mistakes—and not small ones. His most famous work, *The Theory of Relativity,* has been shown to have significant flaws.[25] So why is Einstein still considered a genius? Because his theories were so groundbreaking that "even Einstein's mistakes are informative."[26]

No plan is perfect, but our mistakes can be informative if we're willing to learn from them. This week, we're going to talk about the importance of adjusting and adapting the plan we're currently working on. Now that the Project Team (PT) members have been on board for a week, no doubt they have some ideas that can make everything better—maybe ideas that will require taking an eraser to some of the Core Leadership Team's original plans.

If you're a PT member, we want your input. That's why you're here. In fact, this would be a good week to call your team members and ask if they've seen any mistakes that need fixing. Be ready to adjust and adapt. New ideas aren't a threat, they're a blessing.

"You Moved My Stapler."

As you start working in separate teams it can be hard to keep track of everything that's going on. One Project Team may have a great idea, but their idea unintentionally creates an unforeseen problem for another Project Team. Here's an illustration that helped our church several years ago when we were making big changes but didn't have solid communication systems in place yet.

Imagine that your project is like an office in which all the items are connected wirelessly, but randomly. When you open a desk drawer, it opens the window. When you close the window, it adjusts the thermostat. When you readjust the thermostat, it moves your stapler, and on it goes.

Every time one of your PTs discovers an adjustment that needs to be made—especially a major adjustment—it will probably move someone else's stapler. The only solution is regular, thorough communication. Thankfully, there are productivity apps for that. And texts. And phone calls. And, when issues get really complicated, a sit-down meeting with everyone whose team may be affected.

In my experience, one the main reasons many pastors give

up on team leadership and default to a my-way-or-the-highway approach is not that people were intentionally hurtful (although that happens), but because the leader didn't provide an environment for people to communicate properly. Saying, "You moved my stapler" is one way to create that environment. It's a great way to tell someone that their plan is unintentionally intruding on your plan without accusing anyone of being hurtful or unwise. It acknowledges the problem but puts it in the context of the project, not as an accusation against a person. When you check in with others to ask, "Does this move anyone's stapler?" it allows them to speak up about issues without making them feel like they're being complainers or challenging anyone's authority.

We're all connected in this project. That's what teamwork is all about. Healthy communication is the key to effective cooperation.

DAY 57 (SATURDAY)

There are no team meetings scheduled for the next few Saturdays. Instead, they're open days, so Project Teams can meet as needed.

Today's Big Idea: Something new is happening. This week, we'll spend every day in a different portion of a single story—the extraordinary story of Peter and Cornelius in Acts 10. This passage deserves so much time at this spot in the 100-Day process because it was a watershed moment for change in the early church. In this chapter, a new need arises, God proposes a change, and Peter adapts to meet those needs under God's guidance. It's hard to imagine a situation more suited to what we're hoping to accomplish over the next 40+ days together.

Key Verse: "At Caesarea there was a man named Cornelius, a centurion in what was known as the Italian Regiment. He and all his family were devout and God-fearing; he gave generously to those in need and prayed to God regularly" (Acts 10:1–2).

Passage of the Day: Acts 10:1–8

Thoughts to Consider: Cornelius was a Gentile, but not just any gentile—he was a Roman. And Cornelius was a soldier, a centurion, the commander of an entire regiment. There was no one other than Caesar himself, whom the average Jew would have considered more ungodly or unclean. But Cornelius was a generous, prayerful, God-fearing man, and God wanted Cornelius and his household to know about Jesus. So God sent an angel to tell Cornelius to seek out a man named Peter.

If it feels like changes are coming too fast in your church, try to imagine how big the changes were that were about to hit Peter and the early church. Cornelius was coming! And God had sent him. In some ways, it would have been less confusing if Cornelius had sent his regiment to arrest Peter than sending servants with an invitation to dinner.

As you ponder this passage, ask yourself what's happening with the people like Cornelius who live near your church. There always are such people—good, generous, prayerful folks who don't know where to go. If God isn't guiding them to your church for their next steps of spiritual growth, why not? What can you and your church do to make yourselves available?

DAY 58 (SUNDAY)

Today's Big Idea: God moves Peter's stapler. Before God does something big, He tells His people about it. That was certainly the case in the story of Cornelius and Peter. If we're constantly surprised, angry, or resistant when God does something new, we're not listening when He tells us He's about to move our stapler.

Key Verse: "Do not call anything impure that God has made clean" (Acts 10:15).

Passage of the Day: Acts 10:9–16

Thoughts to Consider: Peter was staying at a friend's house when he decided to go up on the roof for some prayer time. While there, he had a strange vision. Three times, a sheet came down in front of him filled with animals that every Jew knew were unclean. But each time, a voice said, "Get up, Peter. Kill and eat." *Surely*, Peter must have thought, *this is a temptation from the devil, not a command from God.* So he refused the command. But the command *was* from God.

Like our Jewish friends, church folks have a way of functioning. And, also like them, we've been taught that keeping close to those traditions is one of the ways we honor God. But when new people come to faith in Christ, then show up at church, some of those traditions are challenged. Are we willing to accept changes when God brings them—especially when they come in the form of new believers who need our help and patience, not our judgment and stubbornness? Or are we going to keep calling things impure that God has said are pure?

Consider that today. But don't worry. Making God-ordained changes doesn't lead to losing the essentials that should never change. Before our week together is done, we'll see that very clearly from Peter's story.

DAY 59

Today's Big Idea: Peter doesn't hesitate to obey God. When Jesus walked with His disciples, Peter was always the one who ran faster than everyone else—sometimes faster than Jesus, with really bad consequences. But what does the former hothead do in his later, wiser years when God asks him to move faster than he's ready for?

Key Verse: "While Peter was still thinking about the vision, the Spirit said to him, 'Simon, three men are looking for you. So get up and go downstairs. Do not hesitate to go with them, for I have sent them'" (Acts 10:19–20).

Passage of the Day: Acts 10:7–23

Thoughts to Consider: "Do not hesitate," God tells Peter. For a lot of folks, myself included, that may be the hardest part of God's command. *Really? I don't get to think this through for a while?* No. Not this time, anyway. Once Peter knew it was God's will, his only choice was to do it without delay. Most of the time, the Lord gives us a long season to

DO YOU HAVE ANYTHING HOLDING YOU BACK FROM MOVING FORWARD, EITHER ON YOUR OWN OR AS A TEAM? SURRENDER THOSE DOUBTS AND FEARS TO GOD AND TAKE A BOLD STEP OF OBEDIENCE.

reflect, consider, and ponder His will. But sometimes there's an urgency to it. Once you know, it's time to go.

Do you have anything holding you back from moving forward, either on your own or as a team? If so, what do you need to do to surrender those doubts and fears to God and take a bold step of obedience?

DAY 60

Today's Big Idea: God's will defies our expectations. What is God going to do next? The only sure thing is that it won't be what you expect.

Key Verse: "God has shown me that I should not call anyone impure or unclean. So when I was sent for, I came without raising any objection" (Acts 10:28–29).

Passage of the Day: Acts 10:24–33

Thoughts to Consider: Almost everything about Cornelius's story sends up red flags. When Peter walks into his house, Cornelius bows before him like he's a god—because that's what pagans did. Then Peter reminds him that this simple house visit goes against everything he was raised knowing, because "You are well aware that it is against our law for a Jew to associate with or visit a Gentile." But when Cornelius answers Peter's question, "May I ask why you sent for me?" with such a miraculous story of how God spoke to him, Peter couldn't deny it.

When God showed up to do something new, Peter's expectations had to be set aside. How about you and your church? Are there any expectations God may be asking you to set aside? Are they new ways unlike the ways God has worked with you in the past? If so, are you willing to follow God, even if it means doing something you didn't expect?

DAY 61

Today's Big Idea: Peter's mind and heart are changed. Change is hard. Especially for people like Peter (and maybe you) who have spent most or all of their lives serving God in one specific way. It can be hard to serve God in a new way, with new people. But all that matters is that we're serving Him.

Key Verse: "I now realize how true it is that God does not show favoritism but accepts from every nation the one who fears him and does what is right" (Acts 10:34–35).

Passage of the Day: Acts 10:30–43

Thoughts to Consider: Note what Peter did and did not change his mind on. He accepted the monumental changes God had proposed, but he recognized they were based on foundational truths that never change. In verses 36–43, Peter described the events of Jesus' life, crucifixion, and resurrection and how they fulfilled Old Testament prophecy. This was probably the first time the Romans gathered at Cornelius's home had heard any of this.

Changing our minds about long-held ideas doesn't mean losing our faith. If we're making the changes God is leading us to make, they will strengthen our faith. What might God be challenging you with? Are you willing listen to God saying something you've never heard before and respond in ways you never acted before? If so, God will do something He's never done before.

DAY 62

Today's Big Idea: God astonishes His people. God wants to show up in our lives, and He wants to do it through your church body in an astonishing way.

Key Verse: "While Peter was still speaking these words, the Holy Spirit came on all who heard the message. The circumcised believers who had come with Peter were astonished that the gift of the Holy Spirit had been poured out even on Gentiles" (Acts 10:44–45).

Passage of the Day: Acts 10:44–48

Thoughts to Consider: It turns out Peter wasn't the only visitor Cornelius had that day. Peter had some traveling companions. When they saw that the Holy Spirit was being poured out "even on Gentiles," they were "astonished."

God wants to astonish us again. Are you ready to be astonished? If not, why not? Perhaps the only thing more astonishing than the new thing God wants to do is a church that doesn't want to be astonished by God. May that never be true of us. May God astonish us again.

DAY 63 (SABBATH)

CHAPTER 13

Get Ready

Weeks 10–11

B y this time, the Project Teams should have made necessary tweaks to the original plan and should now be working toward their goals. There are no team meetings scheduled for this Saturday or next Saturday, leaving both days open for PTs to meet as needed.

This is a good day for team leaders to ask how team members are progressing on their assignments, what help they need, and how they're doing with their daily devotionals and weekly Sabbaths.

DAY 64 (SATURDAY)

Today's Big Idea: Leadership lessons from the life of Paul.
The apostle Paul is one of the great figures not just in the Bible, but in world history. After having one of the most dramatic conversion stories ever known, he goes from being the leading

persecutor of Christians to being the leading promoter of faith in Jesus. In addition to his faithful life and his foundational writings, Paul's life and ministry are also a great example of what we're doing during these 100 Days—leadership through a time of church transition.

This week, we're going to look at six episodes from Paul's life from the book of Acts to see how we can become better leaders in the church, just as Paul was.

Key Verse: "Set apart for me Barnabas and Saul for the work to which I have called them" (Acts 13:2).

Passage of the Day: Acts 13:1–13

Thoughts to Consider: The apostle Paul didn't start out as the apostle Paul. He began as the traveling companion of Barnabas. Barnabas was one of the greatest of the early disciples. His real name was Joseph, but the other disciples called him Barnabas, meaning "son of encouragement" (Acts 4:36). Barnabas was Saul's mentor. He was the one who convinced the other disciples to receive Saul after his conversion (Acts 9:27), and after being sent to Antioch to determine if the revival there was legitimate, he brought Paul from Tarsus to mentor him (Acts 11–12).

What we commonly call Paul's first missionary journey was actually Barnabas's missionary journey, with Paul as his traveling companion (Acts 13:1–3). But not long after they started out, Paul's ministry became so effective that it appears Barnabas willingly stepped aside to let Paul lead instead of him. Though the Bible never states this outright, it becomes apparent by several pieces of evidence including the fact that, instead of being called "Barnabas and Saul" as they were when they started out

(Acts 13:2), they were later listed as "Paul and Barnabas" (Acts 13:42) or "Paul and his companions" (Acts 13:13). In their culture, the order of names indicates a subtle but important shift, signifying a change in leadership.

Few people ever lay aside leadership as readily as Barnabas did. But that's what we should be willing to do when we realize all our leadership roles are always under Christ's authority, anyway. What does this lesson from Barnabas and Paul say to you about your role in the church? Are you willing to step into leadership, like Paul, when it's your time? Are you willing to step aside, like Barnabas, when that's what's needed? If we really see Jesus as the ultimate leader, we'll be willing to serve or lead whenever and wherever He asks.

DAY 65 (SUNDAY)

Today's Big Idea: Paul builds on a solid foundation. Following the Lord as He does something new does not mean rejecting the foundational principles that got you where you are.
Key Verse: "We tell you the good news: What God promised our ancestors he has fulfilled for us, their children, by raising up Jesus" (Acts 13:32–33).
Passage of the Day: Acts 13:14–52
Thoughts to Consider: The apostle Paul was doing something so new and radical by following Jesus that most of his Jewish contemporaries couldn't go along with it. But that didn't surprise Paul, since he felt the same way until the resurrected Jesus knocked him to the ground and changed his mind and heart. So whenever Paul brought the message of Jesus to a new town,

he started on familiar territory—in the synagogue, reading from the Hebrew Scriptures. From that foundation, he showed how Jesus' message, though revolutionary, wasn't a shift from the Scriptures but a fulfillment of them.

IT'S TIME TO RENEW OUR COMMITMENT TO GOD AND HIS WORD. IF SO, SAY NO TO FEAR AND STEP OUT IN FAITH.

As you consider the current process of change, it's easy to get your eyes on the new things and either be excited by them or angry at them. Instead of focusing on these changes, it's essential to keep our focus on God's will. Are we building on biblical principles? If not, it's time to renew our commitment to God and His Word. If so, say no to fear and step out in faith.

DAY 66

Today's Big Idea: The humble leader. Leaders are not dictators. Dictators are only concerned about themselves. Leaders are concerned for the people they're leading.
Key Verse: "The crowd wanted to offer sacrifices to them. But when the apostles Barnabas and Paul heard of this, they tore their clothes and rushed out into the crowd, shouting: 'Friends, why are you doing this? We too are only human, like you'" (Acts 14:13–15).
Passage of the Day: Acts 14:8–28
Thoughts to Consider: God performed such extraordinary miracles through the ministry of Paul and Barnabas that in some towns the population treated them as gods. But Paul and Barnabas put a stop to it as soon as they realized it was

happening. Paul and Barnabas went back to Antioch, from where they had been commissioned to make this trip, to report to the disciples who were in authority over them.

It's an essential principle of Scripture that no church leader should ever be the final authority. Not only should we not allow ourselves to be treated as gods, but we should all be under the authority of someone else. This is one of the essential aspects of the biblically humble leader. As you contemplate your leadership role in the church, are you willing to walk under authority as much as you're willing to be in authority?

DAY 67

Today's Big Idea: There are no part-time ministers. Are you a full-time paid pastor? No? Your ministry is still essential.
Key Verse: "Paul went to see them, and because he was a tentmaker as they were, he stayed and worked with them" (Acts 18:2–3).
Passage of the Day: Acts 18:1–4
Thoughts to Consider: There's a common misconception that to be a "real" minister, you need to have a full-time job in the church. But most ministers throughout history have not made a living wage from ministry, including the apostle Paul. While he did receive occasional gifts, the primary way Paul earned money was not from ministry, but from making tents (Phil. 4:15–18).

It's not that Paul thought it was wrong to receive compensation for ministry duties. In fact, he argued strongly that it was his right to do so (1 Cor. 9:1–19). But he turned down that right and made his living as a tentmaker so that "in preaching the gospel I may offer it free of charge, and so not make full use of my rights as a preacher of the gospel" (1 Cor. 9:18).

Despite the fact that the church wasn't paying him, no one would have referred to Paul as a part-time minister. The idea that *any* believer was a part-time minister was completely foreign to the early disciples, and it should be foreign to us. If you're a believer, your first call is to worship, serve, and minister. It's not something to do on the side. Even if you don't get to spend a lot of time in efforts you'd consider ministry-oriented, every aspect of your life should be offered in worship and ministry.

DAY 68

Today's Big Idea: Managing your time well. Leaders know how to manage their schedules well. In today's passage, we see an example of how the apostle Paul prioritized his time.

Key Verse: "Paul had decided to sail past Ephesus to avoid spending time in the province of Asia, for he was in a hurry to reach Jerusalem, if possible, by the day of Pentecost" (Acts 20:16).

Passage of the Day: Acts 20:13–38

Thoughts to Consider: Today's passage records an episode in the life of Paul we usually rush right past, but it actually says a lot about his leadership. As Paul was heading back to Jerusalem, he had to head into port for a few days to rest and take on supplies. The most obvious port in the area was Ephesus. It made sense for a lot of reasons, including the fact that Paul had many friends there. But today's Key Verse specifically says he "decided to sail past Ephesus." Instead, he landed in the nearby small town of Miletus. Why? The passage says, "to avoid spending time" in the province where Ephesus was located.

There are times in leadership when we have an urgent, time-sensitive task at hand. While serving God's people is central to ministry, sometimes we have to sail past places and people who will cost us too much of our limited time and energy so we can do what we're called to do. This shouldn't be our default—and it wasn't Paul's normal routine. But if there are time-sensitive tasks we need to get to, it's okay to avoid time-draining relationships for a season in order to get the task done.

As we get closer to Project Day, the sense of urgency will only increase. That urgency should never induce panic, but it will require proper time-management and prioritization. This is not unchristian. It is an essential aspect of wise leadership.

DAY 69

Today's Big Idea: Planning to give. Giving is central to the Christian life because it is central to the character of God. In fact, giving is important enough that it's worth planning for.

Key Verse: "On the first day of every week, each one of you should set aside a sum of money in keeping with your income, saving it up, so that when I come no collections will have to be made" (1 Cor. 16:2).

Passage of the Day: 1 Corinthians 16:1–4

Thoughts to Consider: One of the great, forgotten stories of the New Testament is something the apostle Paul called "the collection for the Lord's people." Everywhere he went, Paul told the churches to start a collection of funds to help the per-secuted church in Jerusalem (1 Cor. 16:1–4; 2 Cor. 8:1–9:15; Rom. 15:14–32). In fact, this is why Paul was in a hurry to arrive in Jerusalem by the day of Pentecost, as mentioned in the narrative about sailing past Ephesus.

Paul told the churches he worked among to collect money every week when they gathered and not to wait until he arrived. Why? Because he knew that planned, purposeful, consistent giving will yield more benefits then a last-minute emotional appeal. This is another example of why planning is not unspiri-tual but one of the ways we practice good stewardship. As you and your team work toward a goal, keep this in mind. If some-thing is worth doing, it's worth planning well.

DAY 70 (SABBATH)

DAY 71 (SATURDAY)

Today is the last Saturday without a scheduled meeting. Again, it has been left open so you can use it for Project Team meet-ings, if needed.

Today's Big Idea: Build on the Rock. This coming week, as we continue to work on our team projects, we're going to explore some Bible passages that convey important biblical principles about planning, building, and preparing.
Key Verse: "Everyone who hears these words of mine and puts them into practice is like a wise man who built his house on the rock" (Matt. 7:24).

Passage of the Day: Matthew 7:21–29

Thoughts to Consider: In this passage, Jesus contrasts two builders—a wise one who builds their house on the rock and a foolish one who builds their house on sand. *But no one builds a house in the middle of the sand, right?* Actually, people do, especially in the Middle East, where Jesus taught. It's the desert, so sand is everywhere! So what is Jesus talking about here? You can build a house in the *middle* of the sand but still anchor it to the rock.

Take a look at the culture around you. Sand is everywhere—shifting values and beliefs that change from year to year, if not from day to day. Just like any house you build in the desert will have sand all around it, any ministry you build will have sand all around it. But you don't have to anchor yourself to the sand. Churches are built within neighborhoods, communities, and cultures that are constantly shifting around us like sand. But even while we live and minister in that desert, we can stay anchored to the rock. We just have to dig a little deeper.

As you work toward building a stronger church, don't be tempted to chase after the latest fads or stay stuck in stale traditions. That's sand. Dig one level deeper to find Jesus again, and anchor everything in Him.

DAY 72 (SUNDAY)

Today's Big Idea: God shows up in His new temple. Why are we so surprised when God shows up? Isn't that what we want and what we're praying for? But when He does, He changes everything. He sure did on the day of Pentecost.

Key Verse: "'We hear them declaring the wonders of God in our own tongues!' Amazed and perplexed, they asked one another, 'What does this mean?'" (Acts 2:11–12)

Passage of the Day: Acts 2:1–13

Thoughts to Consider: This amazing event did not take place in the upper room. Acts 5:42 tells us the disciples spent their days in the temple courts. So on the day of Pentecost, God showed up in courts of the *old temple* to make the believers His *new temple*. After all, a temple is the place where God lives. When God lives in us, we're a temple. The temple is no longer a place, it's a people.

Observers on the day of Pentecost watched this happen and wondered, "What does this mean?" We might ask the same question. What does it mean when we realize we are the temple where God's Spirit dwells? How does that affect what we emphasize when we think of church? Are we treating ourselves and others the way the temple of God should be treated?

DAY 73

Today's Big Idea: A spiritual house. Living stones—now there's an image. There's nothing more dead than a stone, so a stone come to life is truly a miracle.

Key Verse: "You also, like living stones, are being built into a spiritual house to be a holy priesthood, offering spiritual sacrifices acceptable to God through Jesus Christ" (1 Peter 2:5).

Passage of the Day: 1 Peter 2:4–10

Thoughts to Consider: Peter uses the metaphor of living stones on purpose. In the Old Testament, God met His people in a single geological location, the temple—specifically in the Holy of Holies, between the cherubim above the Ark of the Covenant. This place was so holy that only the high priest could go into it on one day a year—Yom Kippur, the Day of Atonement (Lev. 16). So the temple was a holy place, but it was also an exclusive place. God was there, but He was separate from the people.

After the day of Pentecost, all that changed. Now God lives in us, not in a static temple built with stones that you might travel to once a year for atonement. What does it mean to you when you consider yourselves living stones in the spiritual house Jesus is building?

DAY 74

Today's Big Idea: Gathered as a temple. Now that God the Holy Spirit lives in every believer, we have Him with us everywhere, at all times, and that should never be treated lightly.

Key Verse: "In him the whole building is joined together and rises to become a holy temple in the Lord. And in him you too are being built together to become a dwelling in which God lives by his Spirit" (Eph. 2:21–22).

Passage of the Day: Ephesians 2:11–22

Thoughts to Consider: On the day of Pentecost, God showed up at His *physical* temple to make us His *spiritual* temple. From this day forward, God's presence would no longer be restricted to a physical location—not to a single temple or even multiple church buildings. He is present in and with us. When we're alone and need to know God is there and when we're gathered in His name.

DAY 75

Today's Big Idea: Your body, a temple. Temples are places of worship, but we don't worship the temple, we worship the God who lives there.

Key Verse: "Do you not know that your bodies are temples of the Holy Spirit, who is in you, whom you have received from God? You are not your own; you were bought at a price. Therefore honor God with your bodies" (1 Cor. 6:19–20).

Passage of the Day: 1 Corinthians 6:12–20

Thoughts to Consider: The information in the verse today is almost overwhelmed by the attitude of Paul as he delivers it. "Don't you know?" he asks, as if he's shocked that this isn't obvious to them. He's not informing them that they're God's temple, he's reminding them of it and reprimanding them for not acting like temples should act—that is, by honoring the God who lives there. That is the purpose of a temple after all. It exists to honor the deity who lives in it, not to serve the priests who work there.

We, as God's people, are not our own. Our bodies are not ours to do with as we please. We serve the One who lives in us, and everything we do should honor Him. In this passage, Paul indelicately says we shouldn't join those bodies with prostitutes, which was an apparent problem in Corinth. But more than just abstaining from such evil acts, we should ask ourselves every day, "Is the way I'm treating my body the way I want to treat the home where a holy God lives?"

DAY 76

Today's Big Idea: Working together in God's field, God's building. An untended field doesn't grow crops, it grows weeds. We're called to produce crops.

Key Verse: "The one who plants and the one who waters have one purpose, and they will each be rewarded according to their own labor. For we are co-workers in God's service; you are God's field, God's building" (1 Cor. 3:8–9).

Passage of the Day: 1 Corinthians 3:6–17

Thoughts to Consider: Paul wrote this passage to scold the church in Corinth because groups in the church were competing on the basis of which leader they liked better (and you thought your church fought over petty things!). But Paul reminds them we're all in this together. One plants, one waters, but as any farmer knows, no one goes out into the field at night and pulls on the plants to make them grow. The growing is up to God.

In this passage, Paul uses three separate metaphors for the church in a span of twelve words. We are coworkers, we are God's field, and we are God's building. So which is it? We're all three. In other words, we have a lot to do to help the church produce a healthy harvest. And others have a role that nourishes you. Humility is the key.

DAY 77 (SABBATH)

Second Pause Point

If your project will take longer than three weeks to put together, give it the time it needs. But, as we insisted during the first pause, don't stay here too long. Make sure to put your next All-Team Saturday on the calendar as a date for everyone to aim for.

You don't need to have everything perfect before your next All-Team meeting. At this point, momentum is more important than perfection.

STEP 4

Implement the Plan

"His divine power has given us everything we need."

2 Peter 1:3

CHAPTER 14

Bringing It All Together

Week 12

The fourth and final step in the 100-Days process is to implement the plan.

If your project is to launch a new program or different way of doing ministry, this is when you'll start. If your project involves a big event, this is when that will take place. If you're cutting back or consolidating ministries, this is when you'll make those adjustments.

Because there are so many types of projects that a church might launch, there's little I can tell you about the specific one your church has chosen. But this step is part of the 100-Day plan, not because you need detailed instructions, but to make sure your church actually follows through by accomplishing whatever thing you say you're going to do.

DAY 78

Today's Big Idea: All we need. Only God knows what we really need, so we can trust Him to provide it.

Key Verse: "His divine power has given us everything we need for a godly life through our knowledge of him who called us by his own glory and goodness" (2 Peter 1:3).

Passage of the Day: 2 Peter 1:1–11

Thoughts to Consider: "His divine power has given us everything we need." That *everything* sure covers a lot of territory, doesn't it? But take a look at the rest of the verse. That power is given for a specific purpose. It's everything we need *for a godly life*. The idea that God is a magic genie who will empower and enrich us because we say the right words is profoundly unbiblical. God's limitless power is to be used for His purpose, not ours.

If you want to live a godly life, you'll find all the help you need by getting to know Jesus more. It's "our knowledge of Him" that will give us all we need—in our lives and in our church.

DAY 79 (SUNDAY)

Today's Big Idea: Jesus, the mentor. No one in history mentored people better than Jesus. This week, as we continue to work with our team projects, we're going to look at Jesus' mentoring process through the sending of the seventy-two.

Key Verse: "No one who puts a hand to the plow and looks back is fit for service in the kingdom of God" (Luke 9:62).

Passage of the Day: Luke 9:57–62

Thoughts to Consider: Before we look at the sending of the seventy-two in Luke 10, it's important to consider the context. Jesus had been ministering for about two years when He started what is called His third (and final) Galilean tour. Before the tour started, the buzz from His previous tour through the region was already attracting a lot of hangers-on. In today's passage, three different people came to Jesus claiming they wanted to follow Him, but each was given a challenge that at least two of them were unable to meet.

Jesus doesn't want fans, He wants disciples—followers who won't give up when things get hard. What kind of follower are you? This is a question all believers must ask themselves. Would we stay with Jesus if the cost became really high? Because it might. That's who Jesus wants, disciples who will stick with Him, no matter what.

DAY 80

Today's Big Idea: Jesus, the equipper. Once we choose to follow Jesus with all our heart and life, we need to be equipped because we're going to get an assignment.

Key Verse: "After this the Lord appointed seventy-two others and sent them two by two ahead of him to every town and place where he was about to go" (Luke 10:1).

Passage of the Day: Luke 10:1–9

Thoughts to Consider: Jesus had more than the twelve followers who were His closest confidants. There were crowds that came and went as well. But in between the Twelve and the crowds there was a group of seventy-two people (some translations say it was seventy)[27] that followed Jesus closely enough

225

to have been mentored by Him. They had walked with Jesus, observed His behavior, and sat under His training. Then Jesus sent them out two by two, as advance teams to towns where Jesus was planning to minister.

It's important to understand that as much as Jesus was entirely led by the Spirit, it didn't stop Him from planning, mentoring, delegating, and assessing the work. This is why we plan, train, and work in teams in the church. We need each other.

DAY 81

Today's Big Idea: When things go wrong. Just because Jesus approves of our plans doesn't mean they will go perfectly. But when there is a problem, Jesus knows how to fix it.

Key Verse: "But when you enter a town and are not welcomed, go into its streets and say, 'Even the dust of your town we wipe from our feet as a warning to you'" (Luke 10:10–11).

Passage of the Day: Luke 10:10–16

Thoughts to Consider: Jesus knew His life on earth would be ending soon, so He wanted to make the most of the time He had left. The seventy-two were being sent to towns so Jesus wouldn't waste His limited time in places that weren't ready to hear His message. Jesus knew some towns would fail this test of readiness, so He gave His followers instructions about what to do when things went bad. They were told to shake the dust off their feet—a symbolic way of saying, "I'm done with you." This is a helpful practice for any endeavor. Don't dwell on your defeats. Don't wallow in your failures. Shake off the dust and keep walking.

DAY 82

Today's Big Idea: Assessing and prioritizing. No task is completed until it's been properly assessed so we can learn from it.
Key Verse: "However, do not rejoice that the spirits submit to you, but rejoice that your names are written in heaven" (Luke 10:20).
Passage of the Day: Luke 10:17–20
Thoughts to Consider: When the seventy-two were done with their advance tour, they came back and reported their findings to Jesus. With amazement, some of them told Jesus, "Lord, even the demons submit to us in your name." Jesus acknowledged this was wonderful news, then reminded them not to get diverted from the main task, even by such spectacular events. The Key Verse reminds them and us that a great church service, even one in which there is an obvious manifestation of spiritual battles being won, is not as important as souls being brought into the kingdom.

Take a moment today to pause, think, and pray. Are you perhaps in danger of being so busy or so happy with what's happening in your church that it might divert your attention from the main task—reaching people for Jesus? If so, take some time to reflect and renew your commitment to keep focused on the main thing.

DAY 83

Today's Big Idea: Responding with gratefulness. Prayer requests are interesting. We can spend weeks, months, even years praying for something, then after the need is met, we give God a quick *thank you* (sometimes not even that) and go on our way. Jesus never did that. He was always grateful.

Key Verse: "For I tell you that many prophets and kings wanted to see what you see but did not see it, and to hear what you hear but did not hear it" (Luke 10:24).

Passage of the Day: Luke 10:21–24

Thoughts to Consider: After the seventy-two had returned with a good report and Jesus had assessed their efforts with follow-up instructions, He paused to pray. In His prayer, He was so "full of joy through the Holy Spirit" that He was overwhelmed with thankfulness to the Father. After His prayer, He reminded His disciples that they were living in momentous times, great days that the great saints of the past would have been awestruck to see.

We live in such an age ourselves. Jesus is building His church. The Holy Spirit lives inside us. And greater times are yet to come. Are you ready for it? Are you grateful for it? Are you excited by it? I hope so. The mission deserves nothing less than that kind of passion.

DAY 84 (SABBATH)

CHAPTER 15

Practice and Adapt

Week 13

DAY 85 (SATURDAY)
DRESS REHEARSAL

Today's Big Idea: No bigger barns. As we get ready to launch this project, take a moment to step back and consider what we're doing—and what we're *not* doing. When we're working so hard, it's easy to get caught up in the fun, the work, and the hype. That's why there's no better time than right now to remind ourselves that we need to keep Christ's plans and God's glory the center of our focus.

Key Verse: "Watch out! Be on your guard against all kinds of greed; life does not consist in an abundance of possessions" (Luke 12:15).

Passage of the Day: Luke 12:13–21

Thoughts to Consider: Bigger barns. When we stop and think about it, all our plans stack up as nothing more than bigger barns. As George Carlin used to joke about many years ago, it's all just "a place for my stuff." As you spend the day in rehearsal and preparation for the upcoming Launch Day, remember that the point of this event, program, or change is not to become a bigger church or to be better than another church, but to use all your resources to worship Jesus and serve others with greater effectiveness.

Dress Rehearsal

If your project involves a big event or the start of a new program, it's worthwhile to walk through everything in advance. Starting a new discipleship class? Have the curriculum ready to review, walk through the classroom(s) to be sure they're clean, well-lit, and appropriately outfitted with chairs, mics, video, or whatever is needed. Changing something about your Sunday worship service? Bring in everyone who will be involved, including audio, video, musicians, even greeters and ushers—everyone. A big change in your usual Sunday morning routine will bring up issues you can't foresee unless you walk through it first.

Too often, big changes fail because the Sunday we present it to the church is the first time we've *ever* done it. The Sunday morning launch becomes an unintended dress rehearsal instead of a well-presented event. Instead, we need to hold an intentional dress rehearsal so we can make mistakes in an environment where mistakes don't matter, allowing us to adjust, adapt, and fix issues as they arise. This is one of the best ways to assure that you'll have a successful Launch Day.

If the project is about a change in direction, make sure

everyone who is planned to speak about it on Launch Day actually presents their talk today, so all the bugs can get worked out. The more sensitive the subject, the more important it will be to practice your wording with others who can provide an honest critique. If there's video or music involved, play the video and sing the songs for everyone.

Don't worry about getting stale by repeating it too many times beforehand. There will be enough adrenaline on Launch Day to keep the energy high, which is another good reason to be ready in every way you possibly can.

Notes for the Celebration Team

If you're on the Celebration Team for the festivities on Day 100, this is a good time to assess where you are in your progress for that. Be sure to read ahead to Days 99 and 100 for an understanding of what you're aiming for. If you're undecided about what kind of celebration will be appropriate, ask for ideas from the entire group. If you have a solid sense of direction, recruit members to help out. You'll probably be able to use members from other teams, since their projects will be completed by the time the Day-100 celebration arrives.

DAY 86 (SUNDAY)

Today's Big Idea: A heart for God's house. When you mention King David to most Christians, what character trait most quickly comes to mind? Most believers think of David as "a man after God's own heart" (1 Sam. 13:14, Acts 13:22). In today's passage, we will see that heart for God on full display.

Key Verse: "Here I am, living in a house of cedar, while the ark of God remains in a tent" (2 Sam. 7:2).

Passage of the Day: 2 Samuel 7

Thoughts to Consider: David was the king of Israel, but he noticed a problem. He was living in a palace while the Ark of the Covenant—the place where God's presence physically dwelt on earth—was still in a tent. This bothered David, so he told the prophet Nathan about it. Nathan agreed with David and told him to go ahead and build the temple. He even assured David, "Whatever you have in mind, go ahead and do it, for the LORD is with you" (2 Sam. 7:3). But apparently, Nathan hadn't checked in with God first, because that night God told Nathan that David would not be allowed to build the Lord a temple after all.

David's calling was to defeat the enemies of Israel and bring peace to the land (1 Chron. 22:8). Instead, his son Solomon would build the temple. So did David get angry and sulk because he didn't get to do what he wanted to do? No. David thanked God that his offspring would get to accomplish this special task, then he spent the rest of his life assembling the materials to build the temple and training those who would serve there, making Solomon's eventual task a lot easier.

David worked to prepare for a temple he would never get to see because it was more important that the temple got built than that he got to build it himself—or even worship in it. We need David's heart for our church today. We're not building the church for us. If we do it well, it will outlast us and people will be blessed by our work long after we're gone. It's about God's glory, not ours.

DAY 87

Today's Big Idea: Keep the goal in mind. Marathons are long. Eternity is longer.

Key Verse: "Everyone who competes in the games goes into strict training. They do it to get a crown that will not last, but we do it to get a crown that will last forever" (1 Cor. 9:25).

Passage of the Day: 1 Corinthians 9:24–27

Thoughts to Consider: It's amazing to see someone in training for the Olympics. In fact, many scholars believe the ancient Olympics are what Paul was referring to here, since the winners would receive a laurel (leafy) crown as their prize. Yet how often do we see people putting more time, energy, and passion into earthly pursuits that will fade away, yet paying little attention to where they'll spend eternity? It's the same in pursuing church health. The goal cannot be to have a bigger church, a nicer building, or a more well-known ministry. Our goals are bigger and more long-term than that. Always keep the eternal goals in mind.

> THE GOAL CANNOT BE TO HAVE A BIGGER CHURCH, A NICER BUILDING, OR A MORE WELL-KNOWN MINISTRY. ALWAYS KEEP THE ETERNAL GOALS IN MIND.

DAY 88

Today's Big Idea: Called to reconciliation. How many people does it take to make a viable church? According to this verse, two or three will do the trick. Or will they?

Key Verse: "For where two or three gather in my name, there am I with them" (Matt. 18:20).

Passage of the Day: Matthew 18:15–20

Thoughts to Consider: The point of the passage surrounding this often-repeated verse is not about the minimum viable size for a church—although that applies. This verse is actually at the end of a passage about church discipline. It's about the importance of agreeing together when we have to call out a fellow believer on their sin. "Two or three" is a reference to Matthew 18:15–16, which say if a sinful believer won't listen to the one against whom they sinned, "Take one or two others along, so that 'every matter may be established by the testimony of two or three witnesses.'" That, in turn, is a reference to Deuteronomy 19:15, which says, "One witness is not enough to convict anyone accused of any crime or offense they may have committed. A matter must be established by the testimony of two or three witnesses." The emphasis isn't on the size of the church meeting or the "gotcha" of the sin, but on the unity among those who are calling for reconciliation.

Since we are the church, the temple where God's Spirit dwells, we need to hold each other accountable. Today's passage assures us that when we hold each other accountable, God honors it. In this context of reconciliation, "If two of you on earth agree about anything they ask for, it will be done for them by my Father in heaven" (Matt. 18:19).

DAY 89

Today's Big Idea: Count the cost. The cost is everything. The reward is even bigger.

Key Verse: "Suppose one of you wants to build a tower. Won't you first sit down and estimate the cost to see if you have enough money to complete it?" (Luke 14:28)

Passage of the Day: Luke 14:27–35

Thoughts to Consider: Today's verse is not about building a tower, completing your project, or helping your church become healthier. In the context of the entire passage, it's about sacrifice—taking up your cross, giving up everything for the one who gave up everything for us. This life of discipleship will cost you everything. That's the cost we must be aware of. But it's more than worth it, because it's giving up *our* everything to receive *Christ's* everything.

DAY 90

Today's Big Idea: Ending well. This is your last devotional before Launch Weekend. Let's take it all the way home!

Key Verse: "I have fought the good fight, I have finished the race, I have kept the faith" (2 Tim. 4:7).

Passage of the Day: 2 Timothy 4:1–8

Thoughts to Consider: Second Timothy is the last letter we have from the apostle Paul. He wrote it while under house arrest in Rome, awaiting trial before Caesar, perhaps just a few weeks before his death. He was old, tired, and introspective when he sat down one last time to write to a young pastor named Timothy. In his letter, he gave Timothy a charge with several instructions: "Preach the word; be prepared in season and out of season; correct, rebuke and encourage—with great patience and careful instruction" (4:2) and "keep your head in all situations, endure hardship, do the work of an evangelist, discharge all the duties of your ministry" (4:5).

Paul's instruction, of course, is profoundly wise advice that still applies today. Paul reminds us then that he has fought the good fight, finished the race, and kept the faith. Perhaps Paul was recalling the advice of Solomon who, near the end of his life, wrote, "The end of a matter is better than its beginning, and patience is better than pride" (Eccl. 7:8). Sadly, Solomon did not end his run as well as Paul ended his. May we follow Paul's example, as he encouraged us to do, "as I follow the example of Christ" (1 Cor. 11:1).

DAY 91 (SABBATH)

CHAPTER 16

Launch Weekend

If we were running a marathon, we'd be able to see the tape at the finish line right now. For the last few days, even the last few weeks, it may have seemed like it's been one long, hard slog. You've been constantly making adjustments and assessments, constantly saying no to some aspects of the project that just didn't come together the way you'd hoped, constantly wondering if the long-awaited day would ever arrive.

Now it's almost here. It may even feel a little *too* close. In a marathon, this is when the adrenaline kicks in and you find energy you didn't know you had. Your pace picks up. Your legs move faster, kick higher, and even seem to carry you more lightly.

You're almost there!

DAY 92 (SATURDAY)

Today's Big Idea: Give God your second best. Does today's Big Idea seem wrong to you? Like it might be a misprint? Give God our *second* best? *What*?!

Key Verse: "Now go; I will help you speak and will teach you what to say" (Ex. 4:12).

Passage of the Day: Exodus 4:10–17

Thoughts to Consider: When God called Moses to free His people, Moses must have been filled with all kinds of emotions, having been both a prince in Egypt and a Hebrew. As overwhelmed as he was, he could only see his faults. *How can I persuade the most powerful man on earth to give up all his slaves when I can't even speak well?* he wondered. But God told him the slaves wouldn't be freed because of Moses's oratory, but because of God's power, working through Moses's obedience.

Look at the order of events in the Key Verse. In response to Moses's uncertainty, God gave him three instructions. First, go, get the ball rolling and do what I say. Second, after you go I will help you speak. Your words will be eloquent enough for the task. Third, as you go, I'll teach you what to say. You won't just speak eloquently, you'll speak wisely.

That's how God works with us. He doesn't just want us to give what we do best, He wants everything. And He can use it all. It doesn't start with our skills and gifts. It starts with our obedience. Then God does what only He can do, so only He gets the glory.

For some churches, this weekend is exciting and inspiring. For other churches, this might be a weekend with a lot of sadness. You may be saying farewell to a ministry you've loved but that is no longer viable. For still others, it might be a time involving repentance and forgiveness, with a difficult change in di-

> **THE WORK DOESN'T START WITH OUR SKILLS AND GIFTS. IT STARTS WITH OUR OBEDIENCE. THEN GOD DOES WHAT ONLY HE CAN DO, SO ONLY HE GETS THE GLORY.**

rection or a correction of wrong attitudes. Some churches feel overjoyed at what they're doing, while others may feel some sadness, pain, and loss.

Whether you're looking at a weekend of joy or sorrow, hope or grief, don't just think about the task ahead; consider the source of your strength. Are you relying on your own wisdom, skill, and knowledge, or are you surrendering everything to God for His use?

Give it everything you have this weekend. Even if it feels second best, when it's surrendered to Christ, it's more than enough.

DAY 93 (SUNDAY)
LAUNCH DAY

This is it! The day everything has been leading toward.

If your project centers around a big event, it will happen today. If your project starts a new direction or program for your church, it will launch today. May the Lord be with you and your church as you step out on this great, new, God-guided adventure of faith!

Today's Big Idea: Perseverance. Your church is part of a long line of saints through history, people who made decisions others were afraid to make or were not called to make. This week, we'll be reflecting back on this Launch Day by looking at what many have called the *Faith Hall of Fame* in Hebrews 11.

Key Verse: "'My righteous one will live by faith. And I take no pleasure in the one who shrinks back.' But we do not belong to those who shrink back and are destroyed, but to those who have faith and are saved" (Heb. 10:38–39).

Passage of the Day: Hebrews 10:36–39

Thoughts to Consider: Before introducing us to the great people of the faith, the writer of Hebrews quoted from the prophet Habakkuk, who told the ancient Israelites their righteousness did not come from how hard they worked but because of the God they have faith in. Because of this, "We do not belong to those who shrink back." I pray that is true of you and your church. As you step out in faith today, it can be the start of a wonderful new chapter for your congregation, but it's also a chapter in the great story of faith—in the story of those who did not shrink back.

CHAPTER 17

Assessment

Week 14

This week we're going to take time to think, pray, reflect, and assess what happened on Launch Day as we get ready for the final Big Saturday, when we'll share those thoughts, prayers, and reflections with the rest of the team.

DAY 94

Today's Big Idea: Confident assurance. Everyone has their own idea of what faith is. In today's passage, we'll see the only definition that matters—the one written in Scripture.

Key Verse: "Now faith is confidence in what we hope for and assurance about what we do not see" (Heb. 11:1).

Passage of the Day: Hebrews 11:1–5

Thoughts to Consider: For a lot of people, when they hear the word *faith*, the words *confidence* and *assurance* are among the least likely synonyms they can imagine. Many people don't consider faith to be confident and assured; it often feels more uncertain and unreal, maybe even imaginary. But biblical faith is the confident assurance that God *will* do what He said because He has *always* done what He said.

Your congregation has taken a bold step of faith. When you think about what this step means for the future of your church, does it fill you with confident assurance? That's faith. Or are you filled with fear? Certainly, some fear is appropriate. New things can be scary. But like courage, faith is not the absence of fear; it's proceeding despite your fear. That's confident assurance.

DAY 95

Today's Big Idea: The God who exists. Nothing happens without faith. But the object of our faith is what matters most.
Key Verse: "And without faith it is impossible to please God, because anyone who comes to him must believe that he exists and that he rewards those who earnestly seek him" (Heb. 11:6).
Passage of the Day: Hebrews 11:6–16
Thoughts to Consider: This may be one of the most foundational but overlooked truths of the Bible. If we want to have faith in God, "we must believe *that he exists*." Before anything else can happen—before our faith, before the Bible, before the church—there is a God *who exists*.

Since God exists, we don't get to create Him in our image. He refuses to be whoever we want Him to be. God is who He is. Or, as He told Moses, "I am who I am" (Ex. 3:14). Since God actually exists, we can't create Him in our image. But we do get to discover who God is. That's what faith is for—to help us discover, know, love, and serve the God who exists, just as He is.

It's popular in some circles to ask, "Who is God to you?" That's a secondary question at best. Instead, we need to ask, "Who does God say God is?" When we find answers to that question, we've found something worth having faith in. What is your faith grounded in? Anything less than *the God who exists* will not be enough.

DAY 96

Today's Big Idea: The story continues. Are you one of the people who has only been reading the Key Verse in these devotionals instead of looking up the entire passage? (*Gotcha! You thought you were getting away with it, didn't you?*) I know this happens because I've done it, too. But I ask you to slow down a little. Stop and find your Bible, look up today's Passage of the Day and read it. You'll be glad you did.

Key Verse: "God had planned something better for us so that only together with us would they be made perfect" (Heb. 11:40).

Passage of the Day: Hebrews 11:17–40

Thoughts to Consider: If I was told I could only preach from one Bible passage for the rest of my life, it's hard to imagine a better choice than this one. The roster of great people of faith is inspirational, what they endured for their faith is staggering, and what we can learn from them is unfathomable. Yet after all the decisions they made, all the courage they exemplified, and all the persecution they endured, maybe the most shocking statement of the entire passage is our Verse of the Day: "God had planned something better for us." For us! Really?!

As powerful as their testimonies are, and as much as we should honor their extraordinary sacrifices, these heroes of faith knew nothing of the life, teachings, crucifixion, and resurrection of Jesus. There were glimmers of Him given by the prophets, but the reality of Jesus was far beyond anything they could have imagined. But we don't have to imagine it. For us, the story of Jesus is not unknown, it's history. And, more than history, we live with the presence of the Holy Spirit right now. This is why their story is only "made perfect" (complete) when it can happen "together with us."

Their story is made complete in our story, because of Jesus.

DAY 97

Today's Big Idea: Eyes on Jesus. The author of Hebrews keeps on going past the list of heroes of faith in Hebrews 11. The story of these heroes wraps up in the most beautiful way in the first verses of chapter 12.

Key Verse: "Therefore, since we are surrounded by such a great cloud of witnesses, let us throw off everything that hinders and the sin that so easily entangles. And let us run with perseverance the race marked out for us, fixing our eyes on Jesus, the pioneer and perfecter of faith" (Heb. 12:1–2).

Passage of the Day: Hebrews 12:1–3

Thoughts to Consider: *Therefore* is a powerful and important word in the Bible. It points back to what went before and pushes us forward to what's next. This *therefore* is especially important. It reminds us that we're still talking about the Faith Hall of Fame from Hebrews 11, then it tells us what that list was all about. Since we have a role in the next part of this great story of faith, we have an obligation to run our leg of the race well. The only way to do that is to get rid of anything weighing us down—our sins and anything else that might hinder and entangle us. Then we keep running, keep persevering, keep our eyes on the prize. We keep building on what others have already done. And we seek one goal—not our glory or their glory, but Christ's glory. He's the *pioneer* who started everything, and He'll be the *perfecter* who completes it.

DAY 98 (SABBATH)

CHAPTER 18

Celebration Weekend!

Weekend 15

DAY 99 (BIG SATURDAY)
ALL-TEAM ASSESSMENT AND PREP

No great work is ever complete until it's been assessed and the lessons learned have been noted. That's what we'll do on this, the last Big Saturday with the entire team.

This day won't take too long. Unlike previous Big Saturdays, if you start at 9 am, you'll be done by lunchtime.

Your Takeaways

What are your takeaways from this process? The simplest way to discover and catalog them is to give everyone a *100 Days Takeaway Sheet* (found in the Resources and at KarlVaters .com/100Days) that walks everyone through a few simple but important questions, including, *What have you learned about Jesus? What have you learned about the church? How well did this process go?* And *What could have been done better?*

After starting with prayer, have everyone take a few minutes to fill out their *100 Days Takeaway Sheet*. Some will want to take the sheet home to fill out, but try to prevent that. Few, if any, that go home end up coming back. It's now or never.

When almost everyone is done, let those still writing know they can keep writing, but ask the team members to start sharing what they wrote, one question at a time. It's helpful and affirming to hear what this 100-Day process has meant to others. It's also helpful to be made aware of missteps that can be fixed the next time you do this exercise (more on that in chapter 19).

After they're done sharing, ask everyone to keep their *Takeaway Sheets* with them as you move into the final part of your morning together.

Preparation for Celebration

Remember the Celebration Team chosen on Day 43, the folks who have been prepping for tomorrow? This is their moment to shine. By now, they should have all the plans in place for tomorrow's festivities. This will be when they lead everyone else through final preparations for the big day of celebration tomorrow.

Whatever you plan to do tomorrow, take as much time as needed today to follow up from your dress rehearsal last week to rehearse testimonies, shoot video, practice new songs, or anything else that's needed. Close with prayer, then head home, ready for a moment you'll all remember for the rest of your lives!

Today's Big Idea: Finishing the work. There's nothing like finishing well.

Key Verse: "He who began a good work in you will carry it on to completion until the day of Christ Jesus" (Phil. 1:6).

Passage of the Day: Philippians 1:3–11

Thoughts to Consider: If Jesus is in it, nothing can stop it. But we're not the only ones Christ can do His work through. If we refuse, He'll use someone else. How sad it would be to miss out on what God wants to do through your church because you weren't ready to step up. But you *are* ready! You've done your part. Now leave it in Jesus' hands. He'll complete it. And what an end it will be!

DAY 100 (SUNDAY)
ALL-CHURCH CELEBRATION
AND THANKSGIVING

Today's Big Idea: Gratefulness. In Week 3, we looked at a well-known quote from Max De Pree: "The first responsibility of a leader is to define reality. The last is to say thank you. In between the two, the leader must become a servant and a debtor."[28] The first half of this process was about defining reality. The hard work in the second half was servanthood. Now we get to celebrate and say, "Thank You!"

Key Verse: "You will be enriched in every way so that you can be generous on every occasion, and through us your generosity will result in thanksgiving to God" (2 Cor. 9:11).

Passage of the Day: 2 Corinthians 9:6–15

Thoughts to Consider: This passage is not about giving. It's not about seed-faith. And it's certainly not about getting rich. It's about generosity. Take a look at the Key Verse again. "You will be enriched in every way." *Woohoo! Sounds good to me!* But take note of why we're being enriched. It's not so we can keep the treasures to ourselves, but "so that you can be generous on every occasion."

The goal is not to accumulate wealth or blessings, but to nurture a spirit of generosity.

WE'RE NOT SUPPOSED TO BE THE BUCKET WHERE THE FLOW OF GOD'S BLESSINGS STOPS. WE'RE MEANT TO BE A PIPELINE THROUGH WHICH GOD'S BLESSINGS FLOW.

The most joyous, effective, and life-giving Christians and churches ooze generosity. They're not about getting, they're about giving. That should always be the result of receiving God's blessings. We're not supposed to be the bucket where the flow of God's blessings stops. We're meant to be a pipeline through which God's blessings flow.

How to Celebrate

Every church celebrates differently. Some sing loudly, clapping and raising their hands. Some gather for the Lord's Table in reverence and awe. Some throw a party after church with food, games, music, and prizes. Whatever you do, do it today with all your might.

No matter how you plan to celebrate, there are at least three aspects that should be in every celebration day, and they concern the past, present, and future.

First, the past. There needs to be a sincere and significant celebration of the church's history. As we saw in our study of Hebrews 11 this week, remembering, honoring, and building on the faith of the people who went before us has always been central to the Christian faith.

Second, the present. In addition to hearing from the pastor, church members need to hear from some of those who served on the Core Leadership Team and Project Teams about their experience in this process. Their stories of how they've moved from doubt to faith, uncertainty to excitement, and despair to hope over the last 100 days will give voice to those who have not yet made that journey.

Third, the future. Clearly present where you're hoping this process will be taking your church from this point forward. Look ahead to coming weeks, months, and year. Was your project about evangelism? Talk about the people in your neighborhood whom you expect to be part of your church family soon. Are you hoping to rekindle a greater sense of worship? Show them what that might look like in the coming weeks and months. Whatever you've been working toward should not be thought of as ending this weekend, but starting.

When It's Not a Celebration

For some churches, this day might not be a celebration as much as it is a day of remembrance or commitment. If the church's project was to close down or consolidate ministries, it will be a day to honor those who laid the groundwork and give those ministries the respect they deserve. If the project was a change in attitude that required repentance and forgiveness, this will be a solemn day. Even if there are great new things happening, every new thing costs us an old, familiar thing. There needs to be a time to remember, reflect, and honor those who lost something that matters to them. Even those who are celebrating your church's movement into a better future may feel an undercurrent of sadness for days gone by. That should always be recognized and respected.

No matter if it's a day of sorrow, a day of joy, or a day of mixed feelings, it should always be a day of gratefulness.

After the 100 Days

"Do what it says."

James 1:22

CHAPTER 19

Your New Normal

You did it! You, your team, and your church made it through *100 Days to a Healthier Church*! So now what should you do? Take a break? Of course. For about a week. Maybe two.

Then what? Well, the one thing you *don't* want to do is go back to business as usual.

What does a runner do after they've completed a marathon? At first, they rest. They work on recovery. But recovering doesn't mean falling back into old habits. They don't go back to sitting on the couch watching TV and eating junk food—or they shouldn't. Running a marathon is a great accomplishment, but the real goal isn't completing 26.2 miles, it's becoming a more active, healthy person. The marathon served as an incentive to get off the couch, become a healthier, more motivated person. What a shame to waste all that by going back to behaviors that made you unhealthy to begin with.

It's the same in the church. Completing the *100 Days to a Healthier Church* marathon is a wonderful accomplishment.

YOU DIDN'T JUST COMPLETE SOMETHING, YOU STARTED SOMETHING. YOU HAVE A NEW MINDSET, A SENSE OF MOMENTUM, AND A FRESH START.

But if you approached it in the right way, you didn't just *complete* something, you *started* something. You have a new mindset, a sense of momentum, and a fresh start.

Now we need to turn those accomplishments into tools. Let's switch the metaphor from running a marathon to earning a college degree. That is a grueling process, too. But after the graduate walks across the stage and receives a diploma, they don't just go home, frame and hang it on the wall, then keep living the way they did before they started college. The college degree was a *goal*, but once you have it, it's a *tool*. It gives you access to better jobs, higher pay, greater skills, a better understanding of the world and your place in it. A wise graduate uses their diploma to reach higher, deeper, and further than they could go before.

What a shame to earn a college degree, run a marathon, or complete *100 Days to a Heathier Church*, but not build something wonderful on it.

BUILD ON YOUR STRENGTHS

Because of this process, your church has new muscles that may never have been used before. These are strengths you can build on.

Your first strength is that you've learned more about Jesus and His church. You now have a clearer understanding that it's not your job to create a mission for the church. It's your calling to (re)discover Christ's mission for His church and your part in it. Now that you know the truth of that, go deeper. Don't get distracted by your accomplishments. Stay focused on Christ and His mission.

Your second strength is that you're like Nehemiah after he surveyed the wall. You know a lot more about your church, its weaknesses, its strengths, and it possibilities than you did 100 days ago. That knowledge is power. Use it. After all, you haven't rebuilt the entire wall yet.

Your third strength is that you have a team. Don't let that energy or sense of community dissipate. Build on it. Foster those relationships. Ask the teams to think about what they can accomplish next. Now that they know each other better and have worked together so well, turn them loose on other projects, and encourage them to widen their circle to include others.

Your fourth strength is a clearer sense of your church's calling. You did something difficult, and you did it well. Build on that. Did you start a new ministry? Keep it running strong while exploring ways to make it even better. Did you change your direction? Keep moving along that new road, with an eye out for old habits—they'll want to push their way back in again like weeds in the garden. Whatever your project was, it wasn't designed to stop when you hit the 100-Day mark. Keep going.

MANAGING THE ADRENALINE DROP

Life has rhythms—highs followed by lows, an output of energy followed by the need to rest and restore that energy. The higher the energy output, the longer and deeper the recovery time needs to be.

Have you ever noticed that after a big project comes to an end, there's a massive depletion of energy and emotion? Almost every pastor I know experiences that on Sunday afternoon or Monday morning. The output of emotional, social, spiritual, and physical energy on a Sunday is so extreme it needs to be balanced by an equally extreme recovery—also known as a crash.

If you aren't expecting it, that crash can be dangerous. It feels like something has gone wrong. You can feel sad, depressed, angry, even hopeless. The key to managing times like that is to acknowledge that an extreme emotional low is a normal, healthy response to an extreme emotional high. Engage in healthful rest and recovery. Take a walk, play with your kids, tend the garden, have a date night with your spouse. Do whatever allows you to reengage, recover, and slowly ramp up to real life again.

In the church, a time of rest and recovery from the 100 Days marathon should be followed by similar practices. Bring the entire team (not just the CLT, but everyone!) together for lunch after church about a month later. Share stories and lessons learned. Ask, "How has this process changed you, now that you've had the chance to recover and reflect? What were our biggest gains? What could we have done better? And— here it comes—when should we do it again?"

YOUR NEXT 100 DAYS

This process was not designed to be *one and done*.

As you'll remember, the church I've served for more than

twenty-five years developed and used these ideas multiple times, building principle upon principle, getting healthier and healthier, honing our skills so the process became easier every time we did it.

I don't recommend tackling the 100 Days more than once a year, but by the time you gather the team together after a month or so of rest and recovery, it will have been more than four months since the start of the 100 Days, and probably well over six months since you started the initial planning. That means you're about six months away from the one-year mark. It's not too early to start looking at the calendar for next year.

If that seems too overwhelming to even consider yet, I understand. Another go-round may not be needed that quickly. Our church has only approached something this big every five to seven years. But if your church is on the negative side of the Healthy Church Continuum, or deep down the right side of the Life Cycle bell curve, you may need to increase the frequency.

The good news is, the next time you tackle this, it will be easier. You know what's coming. You've already learned a lot. In fact, you might only need to take portions of the 100-Day plan and undertake a shortened version of it. Perhaps just take the pieces that worked best and use those. Do what you can to harness the power of your momentum to tackle a bigger project and get even more done the next time.

If you go through this process once, then a shortened version of it another time or two, what you'll discover is that it stops being a conscious effort and becomes part of your church's normal life. The focus of your church is more automatically about what Jesus wants, not what makes us comfortable. Team-work feels normal and right. Staying static feels less comfort-able than forward motion. Healthy change can be your new normal.

Health carries its own momentum—the momentum of hope.

Afterword

Okay, I've Read the Book. Now What?

If you've finished reading this book for the first time, what should you do now?

Maybe you're a pastor. You read a lot of books. But this wasn't your typical book, was it? It's not meant to be read then set aside. It's meant to be *done*.

If *100 Days to a Healthier Church* seems like something your church could use, the next step is to ask one or two of your closest, most trusted church leaders to read it, too. Or at least ask them to read the first three chapters so they know what it's all about. Let's call them your Exploratory Team to distinguish them from your CLT and PTs.

TURNING ENTHUSIASM INTO ACTION

So when should you start this process? Now.

Seriously, right now. Today. Don't set this book aside and tell yourself you'll get back to it later. Because you won't. If you don't start the process immediately by reaching out to your possible Exploratory Team members today, the likelihood you'll ever do it diminishes with every passing day.

Act now because you're reading this book now. If your

church didn't need some help to become healthier right now, let's face it, you wouldn't have sought out this book and started to read it, much less made it all the way to the final pages. You made it this far! Keep going! Get in touch with your Exploratory Team today.

NEXT STEPS

Have an honest, prayerful conversation with your Exploratory Team about the book. Tell them why you wanted them to read it. Ask what they thought and whether they believe the process is a good fit for your church. If there's serious pushback from this small, trusted, handpicked group, the likelihood of this being successful with a larger team is almost nonexistent.

If they give you a green light, or even a yellow, proceed-with-caution indicator, your next step is to talk about who your CLT members should be. There may be no more important aspect of the entire process than this. The right CLT can set you soaring. The wrong one will sink you, and fast.

Next, recruit your CLT and get a copy of *100 Days to a Healthier Church* into their hands. (Bulk and ministry discounts are available from Moody; email church@moody.edu). Then, while they're reading it, set a start date as described in chapter 2.

As the CLT does their first read-through, take another read through this book yourself, taking note of dates you'll need extra preparation for, possible restart dates after Pause Points, and so on.

Finally, pull the CLT together for Day 1 and begin the exciting journey together toward a healthier church.

RESOURCES

Resources for Day 1

Church Essentials Conversation Starters

The following worksheets are to be used on the first Big Saturday, as seen in chapter 4. They can be copied, front and back, then enlarged to the size of a full page. You can also find full-size, printable versions of them at KarlVaters.com/100Days. This is not an extensive list, so feel free to add other relevant passages as needed.

CONVERSATION STARTER: THE CHURCH

Matthew 16:13–19 ("I will build my church")

_____

_____

_____

_____

Mark 12:28–34 (The Great Commandment)

_____

_____

_____

_____

_____

Acts 2:42–47 (The church in Jerusalem)

_____

_____

_____

_____

_____

Galatians 6:10 (Caring for the household of believers)

_____

_____

_____

_____

_____

James 5:13–16 (Pray for one another)

_____

_____

_____

_____

_____

Romans 12:3–8 (Using your gifts for the body)

_____

_____

_____

_____

_____

Hebrews 10:24–25 (Don't neglect meeting together)

_____

_____

_____

_____

_____

1 Corinthians 12:12–27 (We are the body of Christ)

_____

_____

_____

_____

_____

CONVERSATION STARTER: WORSHIP

John 4:23–24 (Worship in Spirit and truth)

_____

_____

_____

_____

_____

1 Thessalonians 5:16–18 (Pray without ceasing)

_____

_____

_____

_____

_____

1 Corinthians 6:19–20 (Your bodies are God's temple)

_____

_____

_____

_____

_____

Romans 12:1–2 (Living sacrifices)

_____

_____

_____

_____

Matthew 4:8–10 (Worship God alone)

_____

_____

_____

_____

_____

Hebrews 12:28–29 (Reverence and awe)

_____

_____

_____

_____

_____

Psalm 100 (Worship with shouts and songs)

_____

_____

_____

_____

_____

Revelation 4:8–11 (Worship in heaven)

_____

_____

_____

_____

_____

CONVERSATION STARTER: DISCIPLESHIP

Matthew 28:18–20 (The Great Commission)

_____

_____

_____

_____

_____

Ephesians 4:11–16 (The fivefold ministry gifts)

_____

_____

_____

_____

_____

Acts 6:1–7 (Appointing the seven)

_____

_____

_____

_____

_____

Luke 6:40 (The purpose of discipleship)

_____

_____

_____

_____

_____

2 Timothy 2:1–2 (Discipling disciple-makers)

_____

_____

_____

_____

_____

2 Timothy 2:15 (Correctly handle the Word of truth)

_____

_____

_____

_____

_____

2 Timothy 3:14–17 (All Scripture is God-breathed)

_____

_____

_____

_____

_____

Matthew 16:24–25 (Take up your cross)

_____

_____

_____

_____

_____

CONVERSATION STARTER: OUTREACH

Matthew 28:18–20 (The Great Commission)

_____

_____

_____

_____

_____

Luke 10:10–20 (Jesus sends the seventy-two)

_____

_____

_____

_____

_____

Acts 1:8 ("Be my witnesses")

_____

_____

_____

_____

_____

Matthew 5:13–16 (Salt and light)

_____

_____

_____

_____

_____

Luke 4:14–19 (Good news to the poor)

_____

_____

_____

_____

James 2:14–18 (Faith without works is dead)

_____

_____

_____

_____

James 1:27 (Pure religion)

_____

_____

_____

_____

Matthew 25:34–40 ("You did for me")

_____

_____

_____

_____

Luke 10:35–37 (The Good Samaritan)

_____

_____

_____

_____

Resource for Day 99

100 Days Takeaway Sheets

The following worksheets are to be used on Day 99, as recommended in chapter 18. They can be copied, then enlarged to the size of a full page. You can also find full-size, printable versions of them at KarlVaters.com/100Days.

MY TAKEAWAYS

Take a few minutes to write down answers to the following questions. Use the back of this page or extra paper if you need it. Feel free to sign your name if you want someone to follow up with you, but you are under no obligation to do so. Your answers will help the church as we move forward together and will be kept confidential. In the spirit of Christian fellowship, please state your responses honestly, but kindly.

In the last 100 (or 50) Days . . .
What have you learned about Jesus?

_____
_____
_____

What have you learned about the church?

_____
_____
_____

How well did this process go?

_____
_____
_____

What could have been done better?

_____
_____
_____

Acknowledgments

Books don't happen without a great team of people behind them. And this book is no exception.

The first people I need to thank are the congregation members of Cornerstone Christian Fellowship. For twenty-seven years and counting they have been the patient, willing, and encouraging guinea pigs for all my pastoral experiments—both successful and failed. Without their willingness to walk through several seasons of big ministry changes together, none of the ideas in this book could have been tested, tweaked, and improved enough that they could be passed along to others.

Also, for that entire twenty-seven-year span Gary Garcia has been my ministry partner, first as my associate and now as my lead pastor. The success of these ideas is as much a credit to his creativity and support as anyone's.

Mostly, though, I'm grateful to my family. Shelley, Veronica, Matt, and Phil have been through a lot as a pastor's wife and family and they've done so with very little of the drama and trauma that so many other pastors' families endure. And to our newest family additions, Sam, Connor, and Abigail, we're grateful to have you along for the rest of the ride.

Notes

1. Thom S. Rainer, *Who Moved My Pulpit?* (Nashville: B&H Publishing Group, 2016), 130.
2. Tim Suttle, *Shrink: Faithful Ministry in a Church-Growth Culture* (Grand Rapids: Zondervan, 2014), 30.
3. Gretchen Rubin, "Stop Expecting to Change Your Habit in 21 Days," *Psychology Today,* October 21, 2009, https://www.psychologytoday.com/us/blog/the-happiness-project/200910/stop-expecting-change-your-habit-in-21-days?amp.
4. Christine Luff, "How Strict Are Time Limits in Races?," Verywell Fit, May 15, 2019, https://www.verywellfit.com/how-strict-are-time-limits-in-races-2910929.
5. Eleanor Drago-Severson et al., "The Power of a Cohort and of Collaborative Groups," National Center for the Study of Adult Learning and Literacy, vol. 5, issue B, October 2001, http://www.ncsall.net/index.php@id=254.html.
6. Find Dave Jacobs at www.smallchurchpastor.com.
7. Bill Auxier, "Operating on a 'Need to Know Basis' Is Bad Leadership," *EHSToday*, December 7, 2015, https://www.ehstoday.com/bad-leader.
8. Quoted in *Reader's Digest*, September 1947.
9. Chase Replogle, "Bonhoeffer Convinced Me to Abandon My Dream," *Christianity Today,* August 2, 2019. https://www.christianitytoday.com/pastors/2019/august-web-exclusives/bonhoeffer-convinced-me-to-abandon-my-dream.html.
10. Ibid.
11. Francis Chan, *Letters to the Church* (Colorado Springs: David C. Cook, 2018), 45.
12. Max DePree, *Leadership Is an Art* (New York: Dell Publishing, 1989), 11.
13. Rainer, *Who Moved My Pulpit?*, 36.
14. Jim Powell, *Dirt Matters: The Foundation for a Healthy, Vibrant, and Effective Congregation* (Bloomington, IN: WestBow Press, 2013).
15. Tony Morgan, *The Unstuck Church* (Nashville: Thomas Nelson, 2017), 6. See also McKeown, Les, *Predictable Success,* https://getpredictablesuccess.com/about/.
16. Morgan, *The Unstuck Church*, 125.
17. Erin Wildermuth, "The Science of Putting Pen to Paper," April 10, 2018, MichaelHyatt.com, April 10, 2018, https://michaelhyatt.com/science-of-pen-and-paper/.

18. Rainer, *Who Moved My Pulpit?*, 91.
19. Jesse Carey, "12 of DL Moody's Most Profound Quotes About Faith," Relevant, February 15, 2016, https://relevantmagazine.com/god/12-dl-moodys-most-profound-quotes-about-faith/.
20. Larry Gilbert, "How Many Spiritual Gifts Are There?," ChurchGrowth. org, https://churchgrowth.org/how-many-spiritual-gifts-are-there/.
21. Other gifts that are sometimes listed but are not included here include Celibacy (1 Cor. 7:7), Voluntary Poverty (1 Cor. 13:3), Martyrdom (1 Cor. 13:3), Missionary (Eph. 3:6–8), and Hospitality (1 Peter 4:9).
22. Kevin Kruse, "The 80/20 Rule and How It Can Change Your Life," *Forbes,* March 7, 2016, https://www.forbes.com/sites/kevinkruse/2016/03/07/80-20-rule/#7f3d76753814.
23. Apostles, prophets, evangelists, pastors, and teachers (Eph. 4:12).
24. Powell, *Dirt Matters*, 11.
25. United States History, "Cotton Mather," *u-s-history.com*, https://www.u-s-history.com/pages/h1168.html.
26. Andy Stanley, *Visioneering: God's Blueprint for Developing and Maintaining Vision* (Colorado Springs: Waterbrook/Multnomah, 2016), 58.
27. I have described this season at length in my book *The Grasshopper Myth: Big Churches, Small Churches and the Small Thinking That Divides Us* (New Small Church, 2012), so I won't go into detail here.
28. Mark Buchanon, "Why Einstein was wrong about relativity," *New Scientist,* October 29, 2008, https://www.newscientist.com/article/mg20026801-500-why-einstein-was-wrong-about-relativity/.
29. Bill Andrews, "5 Times Einstein Was Wrong," Astronomy, September 14, 2018, http://www.astronomy.com/news/2018/09/5-times-einstein-was-wrong.
30. Some of the translations that say seventy include the KJV, NKJV and NASB. Translations that say seventy-two include the NIV, ESV and NLT. These differences happen because there are an equal number of ancient manuscripts that use each number, and no scholar knows the number for certain. See the note in the NIV Study Bible.
31. Max DePree, *Leadership Is an Art*.

DO YOU LEAD A SMALL CHURCH?

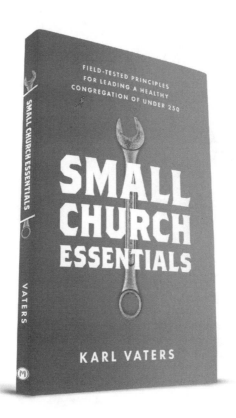

HEALTHY CHANGE
HAPPENS IN COMMUNITY.

Be encouraged by connecting with other pastors and
churches going through the 100 Days—find them at

karlvaters.com

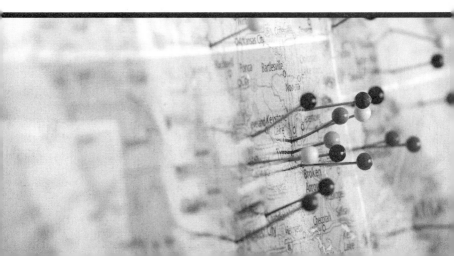

CATCH A. W. TOZER'S CONTAGIOUS PASSION FOR THE CHURCH OF CHRIST

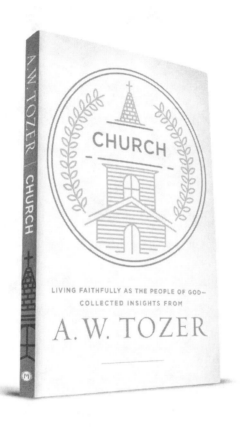